'Three Cheers for the Queen-Lancers-Charge!'

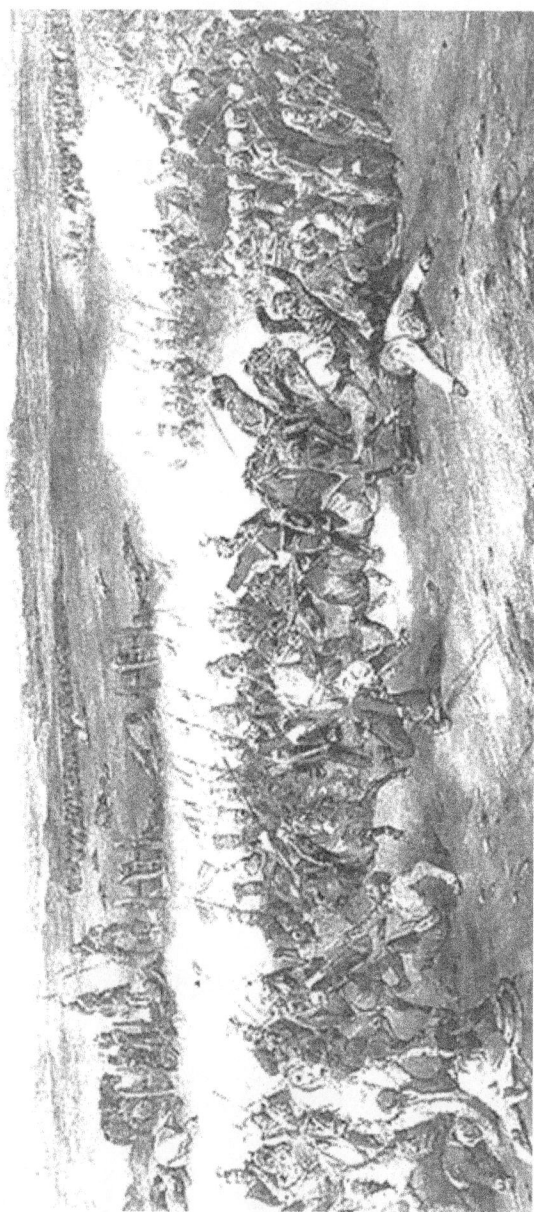

'Three Cheers for the Queen-Lancers-Charge!'

The experiences of a sergeant of
16th Queen's Lancers in Afghanistan,
The Gwalior War, The First Sikh War and
The Kaffir War

W. J. D. Gould

LEONAUR

'Three Cheers for the Queen-Lancers-Charge!'
The experiences of a sergeant of
16th Queen's Lancers in Afghanistan,
The Gwalior War, The First Sikh War and
The Kaffir War
by W. J. D. Gould

First published under the title
Ten Years in India, in the 16th Queen's Lancers.
and
Three Years in South Africa, in the Cape Corps Levies

Leonaur is an imprint
of Oakpast Ltd

ISBN: 978-0-85706-174-4(hardcover)
ISBN: 978-0-85706-173-7 (softcover)

http://www.leonaur.com

Publisher's Notes

In the interests of authenticity, the spellings, grammar and place names
used have been retained from the original editions.

The opinions of the authors represent a view of events in which he
was a participant related from his own perspective,
as such the text is relevant as an historical document.

The views expressed in this book are not necessarily
those of the publisher.

Contents

A 16TH QUEEN'S LANCER IN UNIFORM

To His Excellency,
The Right Honourable
John Douglas Sutherland Campbell
K.T., K.C.M.G.
Marquis of Lorne,
Governor-General of the Dominion of Canada,
&c., &c., &c.
By the Author, Who, as He Has Passed the Meridian, and
is Now Approaching the Limit of His Earthly Existence,
Looks Back With Feelings of Pride, on the Humble Part
He Took, as One of the Old 16th Queen's Lancers, in All
the Memorable Engagements in Which They
Participated in India, and Not the Least of All Does He
Feel the Honour Conferred in Thus Granting Leave to
Issue the Work Under Such Distinguished Patronage.

Toronto, Ontario, 1880.

Preface

The most pleasant memories of my boyhood are clustered around the old family fireplace, in our home in Brighton, England, when my father, gathering us all around him, with occasionally a few intimate friends, recounted such tales of war as often made me desire I was a man at once, in order that I might there and then enrol myself as one of my country's defenders. He had served, I believe, with distinction, in the Tenth Royal Hussars, as an officer, both under Sir John Moore, and the Iron Duke. He was present at the retreat on Corunna, and, as the old man touchingly gave that narrative, I well remember the big tears course down his cheeks, losing all control of himself, his utterances almost ceasing when he pictured the hour when his heartbroken comrades,

Buried him darkly, at dead of night.

This was not all, however. Rising to a pitch of the greatest excitement, his language grew bolder and more fierce as he progressed, bringing us all. through Salamanca, Talavera, Duoro, Orthes, with the Iron Duke, down to the "King-making Victory,"—Waterloo. He may have been too fond of dwelling on his own exploits—the fierce charge on squares—the hand to hand encounters—sabreing this one and then that one—for, as the night's entertainment closed, for such it was considered, his old armchair would be many yards away from its original position, driven by force of arms and legs, depicting this cut at a trooper's head, that point at a breast, this guard from an intended cleaver, as he called it, and I have often since thought, how wise my mother was in her forethought to hide away his sword at such times, for I verily believe, so forgetful was he on those occasions, some damage would be done to arms or legs, in his enthusiasm of description.

It is not to be wondered at, this early training though unintended on his part, had its effect on his son in after life. Intended for the profession of a Land Surveyor, I could brook nothing short of following in his footsteps. The scenes plainly set forth in this narrative occurred mostly in India, during the first Afghan war, in 1839, the Maharatta War, and the subsequent war in the Punjaub, from 1843 to 1846, trying times to the army in India. That country is so full of study, in its ancient buildings, mosques, temples, shrines, and manners and customs, that, I have only cursorily glanced at them, and only when positions and incidents are necessary for the full understanding of my movements, I have no doubt, however, that, by a careful perusal of the whole much interest will be created, and more sympathy excited for the men, who, careless of all else, ventured life to uphold the honour of dear old England.

In some cases, war is too often employed to further ambition, or in adding some coveted spot to an already overgrown empire. With this, the soldier has nothing to do. The English soldier has been often pitted against great "odds, and as there is no retreating in our army, but "to do or die," much more interest centres around him than a soldier of any other country. Kind reader, may I ask you to follow me through, while I endeavour to picture to you such battles as Ghuznee and Cabul, Maharajpoor and Buddewal, Aliwal and Sobraon; and I am sure you will be convinced, as was the old King of Delhi, that men who carried the red cross banner through such actions as these, were really, as he dubbed my old corps, the Sixteenth Queen's Royal Lancers, afterwards, "*The pride of England, and the terror of India.*" ,

Toronto, Ont., 1880.

CHAPTER 1

Regiment in India

Though now fast approaching the valley we all must enter, I feel a certain degree of pride when I remember the Saturday in November, eighteen hundred and thirty-seven, which made me one of Her Majesty's Sixteenth Queen's Lancers. The regiment was then in India, and, as Maidstone in Kent was at that time the centre for all depôts whose corps were abroad, I was sent thither. I am not going to trouble the reader with all the minutiae of drill, horse and foot, always necessary to make a man perfect for his profession, suffice, it was long and arduous, borne with pleasure, so as to get as quickly as possible ready for service abroad. For this purpose I joined, and for this I done my utmost to prepare.

In February, the following year, I, with members of my own and other corps, left Maidstone for Gravesend *en route* for Calcutta. I need hardly detail any scenes which may have occurred in our progress to the port of embarkation. They are often witnessed in England, and once seen can never be forgotten. Preceded by a band playing patriotic airs, brings to the windows and doors all the inhabitants on the line. The soldiers answer cheer with cheer, for their spirits must have vent, and they can read goodwill and Godspeed on the faces of all the people they meet. At this time there was a rumour in England of approaching trouble in Afghanistan. The people as they looked on us, seemed to understand this, and some may have been thinking, "Poor fellows, how many of you will come back, but no matter, they are glad to go, and fight too." British soldiers always are; and

11

in this, a draft for active service differs from those that are sent off in times of peace, when a man would be glad to skulk if he could get the chance.

Arrived at Gravesend, we go aboard the *Lord Exmouth* transport, and as the ship's bell announces the hour for weighing anchor, cheer after cheer bursts forth again from the men all along the docks, caught up by the sailors on the yards, and again by the crowd of spectators ashore, and the ship carries us out of port, away from the land which has seen thousands and thousands of heroes go forth to make Britain what she is.

The confusion for the while is very great, but with willing hands all soon get righted—the golden rule on board a troop ship is rigidly adhered to, *A place for everything, and everything in its place*. All now settle down to life aboard. On the fifth day out, our ship in a fog struck a rock, sprung a leak, and we were obliged to put into Plymouth Sound; in three days all was again righted, and we started on our voyage. Nearing the Cape de Verde Islands, we pass the line, and as it may be interesting I will here give a description of the customary honours paid to old Father Neptune while passing the equator. All who had not crossed this imaginary line before, which, of course, in our case were few, had to be shaved, or pay a fine to Father Neptune. The boatswain acted as the redoubtable father; over the side under the bowsprit; he first challenges, then comes on board attended by his sea-nymphs, riding on a gun rigged for him; a board is placed over a large tub of seawater; the men who have not paid their respects before—crossed the line—are ranged along the board, lathered with a tar brush, and shaved with an old iron hoop, then soused into the tub of salt water, amid roars of laughter.

Passing Cape de Verde Islands, the first land we saw for six weeks, we were becalmed—not a breath of wind, the heat in the tropics intense. We spent some of our time in fishing; we caught several *beneta*—a beautiful fish—and some dolphins. We now got a good breeze, rounded the Cape of Good Hope far to the west, and entered the Pacific Ocean. Here we encountered some rough weather, when calmed we caught many albatrosses with pork; this is a splendid bird, measuring eighteen feet from tip to tip of wing, all white, and strange to say, when they are brought on deck, they get giddy, and cannot fly, though free to do so. Passing the barren, rocky islands of Saint Pauls and Amsterdam, we approach the Indian Ocean. Just before entering these waters, the sky had every appearance of a storm, and sure enough the day after we noticed the indication, we encountered a perfect hurricane, carrying away fore-mast, main and mizzen, long boat, our good cow and sheep, and seven pigs, leaving us a perfect wreck.

This lasted two days and nights. We were drifted about one thousand miles away from land, but Captain Warren rigged jury masts, and the day after we sighted a French ship. After passing signals the captain promised to keep by us till we got to the Mauritus. In five days we sighted the Isle of France, here our vessel was overhauled, everything made right to enable us to continue our voyage. All went well until our arrival at the Sandheads off the mouth of the Hooghly River. Here we signalled for a pilot, and soon made the Hooghly, one of the many branches of the Ganges. Passing Tiger Island, many of the natives came off in dinghies, almost naked, to see us. At first we supposed they were women, from having their hair tied up and fastened with a comb on the top of the head. Diamond Harbor was also passed, until we made Fort William, where we anchored. Just five months' sail from England.

When viewed from on board ship, Calcutta, in the bright morning sun, presents a beautiful picture; the city rises high from the edge of the grand old river with imposing majesty. The marvellous line of architecture in every possible variety of form—countless numbers of temples, small and great, and overtopping these, fortress-looking stone and marble palaces—certainly nothing could be more unique than such a first glimpse under a bright sun, and blue sky, of forms so fantastic—brightest lights and shadows numberless; of balconies, verandahs, towers, cupolas, projections, recesses, galleries endless and undescribable; and again, the costume of the natives who came to see us, merchants, nabobs, Chinese, Parsees, people from Bengal, Bombay,

Madras, in fact from every place under the sun one would imagine.

On the following day we disembarked, and proceeded to Chinsura, about twelve miles along the river. This is a large fortress, built by the Dutch. As we proceeded we saw the governor general's palace, built of white marble. Garden Reach must be a most beautiful place to reside, with its villas on the banks, and delightful palaces, and cocoanut trees sloping to the water's edge. It is here generally the European merchants reside. We found the Dutch fortress or barracks a most spacious building, with lofty rooms, each capable of holding one hundred men. The Twenty-sixth Cameronians, and part of the Forty-ninth Foot were here awaiting orders for China, and detachments of the Third Light Dragoons, Thirteenth and Forty-fourth Infantry, waiting orders, as we ourselves were also, to proceed up the country to join their respective regiments.

While waiting at the fort, before proceeding to join the regiment, the cholera broke out among the troops, and for the time it lasted we suffered severely—as many as twenty falling victims in one day. In July we received orders to proceed up the Ganges to Cawnpore, embarking on the fifteenth in large boats with thatched roofs, looking like floating houses; each boat's crew consisting of seven sailors in charge of a *jemida*, or captain. I learned after these men were pressed from the surrounding villages, as many of them ran away, and, indeed, no wonder, for the work must have been very laborious, pulling by ropes along the bank, and at this season the current was all against them, as the river had lately overflowed its banks. Nearing Ghazapoor, we encountered one of those severe typhoons, so common, and which come on so suddenly in India. This one broke with terrific force, capsizing the boat I was in, and giving all hands a baptising in the raging river. The sergeant-major, his wife, and myself were washed to a sand bank.

One young lady, going up the country to join her father, a captain in one of the regiments, was lost—we suppose, as the river was full of alligators, she was captured by one of them, The *jemida* and his crew we never could find; but suppose they ran

14

away. The other boats had gone ahead, and as soon as I found my way clear—being a good swimmer, I shot out for the bank, ran along for more than a mile, until I reached the rest. They sent back aid and rescued the man and his wife. If this was to be my experience of the Ganges, give me before it half a dozen ocean voyages.

The beauty of the scenery along the Ganges is hard to describe—fertile valleys innumerable, indigo plantations—here and there flocks of beautiful parrots; monkeys by the hundreds, capering about, particularly in the Tarmarand trees, pulling and throwing cocoa-nuts about, and as we moored at night the trees would be swarmed, grimacing and yelling, such an unearthly noise—add to this, all around seemed spotted with fire from the innumerable fireflies, while the chorus the monkeys made, and the noise from the flocks of flying foxes, almost scares a stranger. As the face of the country alters, so the extent of the overflow can be best seen. In some places, where the land is low, five or six miles in breadth is covered with water; in others between high rocky banks, confine its course, and here the flow of water is very great, trying enough on the boats, and the unfortunate men pulling them.

At Benares we stayed one day. This is the holy city of the Hindoos, as Jerusalem to the Jews, or as Mecca to the Mahommedan. This city contains from nine hundred to one thousand temples, and thousands of images of the many gods worshipped by its people. The highest ambition of the Hindoo devotee is, although he may be tottering with age or sickness, and almost crawling on the earth through deformity, to visit the shrines at Benares, and walk for fifty miles around its sacred territory. Here they come from all parts of India, as it is considered a sure passport to glory to die within it. The temples have all their gods; some of them ugly looking monsters. The people prostrate themselves and strike a bell, which is in every one of them, and then depart. At certain great festivals, thousands assemble from the city on the banks of the river—a great bell is struck—horns are blowed by the priests, then these fanatics, thousands of them, men, women and children, rush headlong into the deep water,

15

THE MONKEY TEMPLE AT BENARES
(FROM ORIGINAL EDITION)

and hundreds are drowned.

From Benares we went to Allahabad. Here the waters of the Jumna unite with the Ganges. This is also considered a very sacred place; the water from here is taken to all parts of Hindostan in bottles, as holy water. It was here Lord Clive gained such a decisive victory over the Great Mogul of Delhi, as secured Bengal to the East India Company. From Allahabad, we proceeded to Cawnpore, where we arrived on the fifteenth of October. Disembarking, we went into tents, and soon after joined the camp waiting for us. I merely rambled through this city to get some things at the bazaars. The goods were all exposed to view without shop-windows, as at home. The merchant sitting, tailor-fashion, on the boards. Of money changers there was plenty; heaps of gold and silver coin on small tables. The sugar dealers, or rather confectioners, had large coppers boiling, making *jillavies*, a mixture of butter and sugar. There is also a goodly number of *bungalos* and gardens, residences of rich merchants.

Early in the morning, generally at three o'clock, when the march of troops commences, one is surprised at the number of animals required for the several conveyances. Elephants and camels for tents and baggage; bullock *hackeries* for women and children. Married soldiers are well provided for in India, a fund provided by Lord Clive allows every woman five, and every child three *rupees* per month, almost enough to keep them comfortable. The first day's march was over by eight o'clock in the morning, when tents were pitched, and breakfast prepared by black servants. After this, what time you don't want for rest may be spent as one chooses.

The weather being intensely hot, we found shade under plenty of orange and mango trees, occasionally issuing from cover to shoot pigeon, or chase monkeys. Birds of all plumage filled the air with their beautiful notes; the mocking bird was particularly favourable to us soldiers, as numbers of them followed us. We were now on our march to Meerut, where the head quarters of my regiment were stationed, and I felt more than anxious till I joined them. On the fourth day from Cawnpore we halted under a famous Banyan tree, which on some previous occasion had shaded five thousand troops. This idea may seem preposterous; but when you take into consideration the length of time it has been growing and spreading, it seems simple enough, each branch on rising a certain height, drops, takes root again, rises again, and again drops, and so on for ages, until from the one parent root, branches and roots covered acres of ground.

Meerut is at last reached on the 14th of November. This is a frontier station. The military cantonments were extended on an open plain three miles in length. The most beautiful barracks, like villa residences. The English church side by side with the theatre, standing between cavalry and infantry lines. Here I found my regiment, and having acted as provost *en route*, I was introduced by Captain Havelock—afterwards general—who came out with us, to his brother Charles, who was adjutant of our regiment.

Now commenced my service in India in earnest. What was rumoured in England proved here a fact, of an army being got ready for Afghanistan. Captain Havelock left to join his regiment; all who had known him, and experienced his kindness on board, and on the march to this station, felt the parting much, as he was invariably kind and very good to all his men.

CHAPTER 2

Battle of Ghuznee

The order for marching for active service at last came, and on the 25th November, we left Meerut to join the force assembling under General Sir Henry Vane, to proceed to Afghanistan to replace Shah-Soojah on the throne usurped by Dost Mahomet. The force he was to have under him consisted of the entire Meerut division—three brigades of cavalry—three of artillery—and three regiments of infantry—the 16th Queen's Lancers were commanded by Colonel Robert Arnold, and were eight hundred strong.

Our route lay through the City of Delhi, so famous in all Indian annals—the city, beautiful as we passed through, must have been almost a paradise before being sacked and plundered by Nider Shah, the Persian adventurer—he and his army are reported to have carried off one hundred and fifty camel loads of treasure, consisting of gold and silver—jewels and articles of great value. The principal street running through the city is called Chan-de-la-gore, a stream of water dividing it all though, with orange and *tamarand* trees on each of its banks,—the bazaars were crowded with people, and goods for sale, chiefly jewellery, silverware, and in some, costly apparel, such as the gorgeous Cashmere shawl, and elegant Persian carpet. I must reserve a full description of Delhi to another part of my experience.

The army, under the commander-in-chief was to assemble on a plain five miles from Delhi, and was to number thirty thousand men of all arms. To this rendezvous we marched. The following day we were reviewed before the King of Delhi, he and his Court could not help but be well pleased with the dashing fellows that passed before them, we then continued our march through the protected Sikh States, until we arrived at the Sutlej River, where we halted until a formal permission to proceed was secured from the Maharaja Runjiet Sing in order to pass through his country, the Punjaub. At this time the *maharaja* or king was very powerful, had a large army, with four French generals in his service—Avitavula—Ventura—La Court and Belasses. Permission was granted to pass through to Upper Scinde.

At this distance of time, and looking back on the misery endured in that dreadful march. The country is very sandy—the heat is intense, and days without water. Eventually, after much suffering we reached Attack, or the upper waters of the Indus near Hyderabad. Here we halted a while and refreshed, Sir Harry Vane refusing to proceed through those sterile mountains of the Hindoo Koosh without strong reinforcements to keep his communications open with the rear. General Sir John Keene was ordered up with a force from Bombay, consisting of the 4th Light Dragoons, accompanied by artillery and infantry. Sir Harry Vane, through illness, not feeling able to continue in command, resigned, left for home, but died on the passage.

Crossing the Attack River, on the 15th January, new horrors presented themselves thick and fast; the country still continued very sandy, in fact a desert, no appearance of anything around or ahead of us to instil a hope of comfort; again we had great suffering though want of water. Before we proceeded far it was deemed advisable to send back the elephants, and as for the poor camels they dropped off by scores for lack of food, the tents and a great part of the baggage and forage had to be burnt, the men were attacked with dysentery in its worst form, and many died. This may be allowed was an auspicious commencement of my military life in India. Did our men regret, or get faint-hearted?—No. Did we think of home and all its comforts, and the little thought there of the endurance of her soldiers?—we did; but there was no such thing as repining—though we did think too much was expected. Endurance has an end,—and that those who plan such designs, should be obliged to accompany the army through this country, and put up with, and be content with all we had to put up with, without a sign of discontent,

Through much suffering we reached the valley of Shaul, through Beloochistan to the entrance of the Bolan Pass. This gradually rises to an elevation of something like 12,000 feet. It appears as if some convulsion of nature—and I have no doubt of it—split the mountain completely in two. At this time no Doctor Russell or Archibald Forbes ever thought of such a mad freak as to accompany an army—they are free to do so now, because perhaps, in many particulars the army is better equipped and provided for—comforts unknown to us, are supplied now—and so it should be—for the soldiers who fought for England half a century ago, must have been hardier, and possessed of greater endurance, to do as they did on hard rations, and often half rations, with less formidable arms, no possible comfort, and discipline almost carried to extremes.

In passing through the valley we were obliged to dismount, and actually pull or drive our horses along, they were so used up. While camped in the Pass, Lieutenant Inverrity strayed from his regiment, was surprised by a party of Beloochees, and cut and hacked to pieces. After losing many horses and men, and having undergone much privation and suffering, we arrived at Candahar, here we rested to somewhat recruit our health—procure fresh horses, and here we crowned Shah-Soojah. The rest we had here was very acceptable, and after all we endured on the sandy plains, and through the valley—the refreshment, plentiful here for the inner man—was in abundance—grapes and pears were very large, and vegetables without stint—the cabbage here is about the size of an ordinary wash-tub, very sweet and good. The inhabitants vied with each other to please us, as we were the first British troops they ever saw. The city, like all places of note in India, is very attractive, the houses flat-roofed—any woman you meet in the street all belong to the low caste, very heavily veiled—the High caste women are never seen out.

On the 4th of June we broke up camp and started for Ghuznee, our way lying through the Bolan Pass. As we approach, its appearance is formidable, the mountains at each side seem to reach to the clouds, they have an ascent of 14,000 feet. Arriving at Ghuznee on the 21st July, we observed on the hills, Hadjie Khan the commander of Dost Mahomet's army encamped with twenty thousand men. Ghuznee is strongly fortified—cut out of solid rock, on the slopes of a hill, surrounded by a moat. As the enemy commenced firing on the 22nd with heavy shot, our commander thought better to move the camp back about two miles.

On the morning of the 23rd, we moved up at three o'clock, and got into position. One division of cavalry opposite the gate on the Cabul road; one part of our force moved off to our left, to watch the enemy on the hills, and make a feint attack on their position on the opposite side, so as to draw their attention from us. We were occupied in placing batteries so as to command the gate: at the same time Colonel Thompson, of the Engineers, was laying a chain cable to throw a bridge across the moat. When this was accomplished, a mine was laid under the stone buttresses, and at a quarter to six o'clock the mine was opening, and up went the gates with a terrific crash. The storming party, consisting of the 13th Light Infantry, under Colonel Robert Sale; the 2nd or Queen's, under Sir Thomas Wiltshire; when the bugle sounded, commenced their attack under a heavy fire—the 13th had the honour of leading.

The enemy everywhere made a terrific resistance. Colonel Sale was knocked off his horse and trampled upon, still he ordered the bugler to sound a retreat, instead of which, whether intentional or not, the advance was sounded. Nothing could daunt the ardour and bravery of the men. They soon gained a footing inside, where hand to hand encounters was carried on in its most relentless form, and in half an hour, both regiments were firmly established inside the walls. By daylight the British flag was mounted on the citadel, many of the enemy having thrown themselves therefrom, rather than surrender, to the moat below, a distance of 150 feet.

We were ordered to enter and seize the horses, which were running wildly without riders, which we did after some hard work, and brought them to the prize agent outside. We were annoyed, however, very much, through having to encounter the worst of firing, as many of the Afghans popped at us from loopholes and windows in every street of the city. When the sun rose on the hills the Infantry could plainly be seen ascending the greatest heights of the citadel, far above the city; here they got into the bank, and loaded themselves with money. Many of the enemy were trying to escape to the valley away on our left; these, and the force on the mountains, kept our troops in that direction busy. By 2 o'clock, p. m., all was over, and Ghuznee was in possession of the British.

When all opposition ceased, and one went through the city, now filled with sounds of wailings, he cannot but be struck with the dreadful havoc war brings with it. This was my first general action, and although when in the heat of it, I felt no pity for anyone, at least I cannot remember feeling so, still, when the desolation is complete, and you are met everywhere with its sad effects, property destroyed, mutilation of brutes, horses, camels, &c., dead, and writhing in pain from wounds; wounded men and women everywhere begging for mercy or succour, the dead piled all round, the most hardened must give way to sadness. Shah Soojah, our newly crowned king, was busy on our right, hanging and shooting traitors, some of them leading chiefs who had fallen into his hands.

The whole of the 24th was occupied in burying the dead, and on the following day Hadjie Khan came in, and gave up his sword, a beautiful one, the hilt studded with costly gems; for its possession the officers had a race, which was won by the 4th Light Dragoons. The horses captured, all of them valuable Arab or Turcoman were sold by auction, the proceeds appropriated as prize money.

We halted here three weeks, sending out detachments to scour the country for Dost Mahomet's troops. During this time the inhabitants began to be much familiarized to us, and brought on all the supplies we required. We had much trouble, however, in striking bargains, as they do not speak Hindoostanee; but this we did experience, their great liking for us, over the regular Indian troops, our *sepoys*.

On the 2nd February we received orders to prepare for an advance on Cabul. Colonel Cureton was to proceed with two troops of the 16th Lancers and three troops of heavy artillery as an advance, my troop was one of these. On the 3rd, our way lay through high rocky passes, these we had to ascend, not without great difficulty, and on the second day's advance, we came upon four guns planted so as to command a lead in the road. They were loaded, but abandoned. The artillery unloaded them, blowing up the tumbrels, one of the men through accident having his arm blown off. Our march through the gorges and passes was very tedious till we arrived at Cabul, the capital.

As we approached, the inhabitants gathered to greet us, and a right hearty welcome we got, as we were the bodyguard of the king, and the first British soldiers they ever saw. Encamping opposite the main gate, we were supplied with all the dainties of the city—milk, bread and fruit in any quantity. They were very kind, particularly to us horsemen, and would take no money in return. As we had two days before the headquarters with General Keene would arrive, I had many a stroll through the city and the bazaars; but as Cabul has come into great notoriety since I was there, and has been described over and over again, I will not enter into much detail. The inhabitants are mostly Mahomedans, some Armenians and Hindoos, who are generally merchants. They strike one on first appearance with the Jewish type of features, and it would not, perhaps, be risking too much to say they are descendants of one of the lost tribes of Israel, for we read in the 9th chapter, *1st Book of Kings*, that King Solomon gave to King Hiram, in exchange for wood brought to build the Temple, twenty cities, and he called them the land of Cabul unto this day.

We found at that time plenty of Russian money and goods, showing that that nation then, as lately, had an avaricious desire for possession of the country. The people are mostly of fair complexion, and the women are certainly very fine looking, of the Circassian type. After the arrival of General Keene, we commenced forming batteries and trenches. One sad occurrence overtook our regiment, which caused more profound regrets more heartfelt sorrow, than anything else that could possibly befall us, and that was the death of our old esteemed Colonel Arnold. He was fully half a century in the army, loved his men as a father his children,—a splendid cavalry officer, six feet two inches high. Feeling he could not live much longer, he desired to see his regiment before he died. His cot was brought out, he, having all the appearance of death, propped in it.

The regiment was formed on foot, three deep. We then marched slowly past him, giving one sorrowful look, and that a long one, at our poor colonel. Tears filled all eyes. The officers, as their troops passed, fell in at the side of the cot, and when all had passed through, his lips were constantly moving, seemingly muttering some farewell, he audibly, exclaimed "My poor, dear fellows," fell back and expired. His remains were interred with great military and Masonic honours in the Moslem cemetery.

While we remained at Cabul, his grave was often visited, and many a deep regret was expressed over it. While looking about the many stones marking the place of the departed, I was struck with a stone erected to the memory of two English people, dated 1662. How they came to Cabul, or anything about them, no one could inform me. It was certainly an early period—nearly two centuries ago.

The object of the expedition became now a matter with which everyone was acquainted. Shah Shojah, an ally of our Government, was placed on the throne, to counteract Russian ambition to our Indian Empire. Russia at the time was engaged in war in Circassia.

Towards the end of September, leaving General Elphinstone with a small force to protect the king, the remainder of the troops, under Sir John Keene, left Cabul on our march towards India, *via* the Guddulek and Khyber Passes, taking Dost Mahomet and his commander-in-chief as prisoners of war. The 16th Lancers acting as bodyguard, had also the care of the prisoners. The force now consisted of my regiment, two troops Horse Artillery, one regiment native infantry, with Skinner's Irregular Horse. Our route lay towards the Gillum River; this our horses had to swim. Colonel Cureton, now commanding the

16th, nearly lost his life. As his horse rolled over in the current, one of his men ran along the bank, and, although heavily booted and spurred, jumped in, caught him by the hair, and thus pulled him out.

The first week in October we entered the Khyber Pass, and although the mountains on both sides swarmed with Khyberees and Ghysaltees, they made no hostile demonstration, and allowed us to pass. Had there been any attempt at a rescue, we had previous orders to shoot the king, now captive, and his commander-in-chief. After a tedious march through the rugged pass, we reached the fort of Jumrood, which stands at the mouth of the Plains of Peshwa, and the French General Avitavula was governor of that district for the king of the Panjaub. He came to meet us and pay his respects to Sir John Keene, and escort us through the Province of Peshwa. Here we halted five days, during which time I saw thirty bodies hanging in trees, and was informed that was the punishment meted out by the French general to robbers, mostly hill tribe men.

The Panjaub is a very fertile country, abounding in game, wild boar, deer and pea fowl. We killed no bullocks on our march, out of respect to the inhabitants, as they are mostly Brahmins and worship the bull as sacred. We crossed the Sutlej, the British boundary, and arrived at Meerut in complete rags, horses and men worn and jaded; what clothes we had, patched with sheep and goat skin. We left just sixteen months before, in all the ardour of youth, bright scarlet and gold lace, now sad looking spectacles—brown as mahogany, and faces covered with rough hair.

Our losses during that time were very great. Besides our colonel, we left two hundred officers and men behind, almost all through hardship and fatigue. The loss during the campaign in horses alone was 3,000, in camels 1,400. On arriving at Meerut we subscribed a week's pay each, had a handsome marble monument erected to our departed comrades in the churchyard. We now required some rest, and we had it. As the recruits from England were awaiting us, they relieved us from duty for awhile, and having a large amount of pay and battier money due us, we gave ourselves up to rest—recreation such as one can have in a hot country—and general enjoyment.

The area of India is about 1,558,254 square miles. From the northern extremity of the Punjaub to Cape Cormoran in the south, it measures 1830 miles; its greatest breadth is about the same; its population is about 270,000,000. The prevailing religions are Buddhism, Brahminism, and Mahommedism. The first contains many excellent moral precepts and maxims, but practically it is a religion of Atheism. The doctrines of merit teach its devotees to believe in the transmigration of souls. "If any man sin "it tells him to build a pagoda, or carve an idol, it threatens him with degradation into a soulless brute, it leaves him without hope, without a god in the world. Brahminism is idolatry in its most debasing forms. It has three hundred millions of gods, but no creed; sun, moon, and stars are deified; sticks, stones, or a lump of clay smeared with red paint, are convertible into objects of superstitious reverence.

The rites which it imposes are impure, and sensual. Mahommedanism differs from the other two in that it is not idolatrous. It professes a reverence for the supreme being, but like all human systems of religion it is unsatisfactory, it recognizes no divine mediator between God and man; maintained by the sword, it exercises a cruel and despotic sway over the minds of its votaries, it is remorselessly intolerant and persecuting, deprives men of liberty, upholds slavery and polygamy, and degrades women to the level of the brutes. It is one of the most powerful anti-Christian systems in the world, holding under its iron sway one hundred and seventy-six millions of the human race. A tradition prevails that Christianity was first introduced by Saint Thomas the Apostle.

However that may be, when the Portuguese arrived in India, *a. d.* 1500, they found a large body of professing Christians with upwards of a hundred churches, who traced their history for thirteen hundred years through a succession of bishops to the Patriarch of Antioch. The Hindoos resisted all attempts of the Portuguese priests to convert them to the Roman Catholic faith. "We are Christians," said they, "and do not worship idols." Many of them were seized and put to death as heretics. Many missionaries went to India in the sixteenth and seventeenth centuries. But the East India Company did not encourage the mission work, as they seemed to keep the natives ignorant of Christianity, and by keeping the Hindoos and Mahomedans antagonistic to each other it aided them in their conquests and growing power. But recently a great many colleges have been built in Bengal, Bombay, and Madras by rich Parsee merchants, and the Hindoo youth are deriving great benefit, and since steam has opened up the rapid passage and the voyage shortened through the Suez Canal they have more frequent intercourse with the European, his manners and customs.

CHAPTER 3

44th Foot Cut to Pieces

I have often been ashamed in India, when called a Christian, to see an officer or a man under the influence of liquor. Both Mahomedans and Hindoos are very abstemious—never touching anything that intoxicates. I had now more proof of this than at any other time, there being so many attendants allowed soldiers, indeed as many followers as men, I could well judge their aversion to drink. Of all the native cooks, *belt-wallas, scyses* for horses, and grass-cutters, I never knew one to drink ask them, they grimace and turn away.

During the time we were recruiting our strength the Hindoos had a festival called the *Mahoram*. They assemble by thousands from all parts, with richly dressed elephants and camels, and gorgeously dressed Princes and Nabobs. The common folk go through a sort of sham-fight with bladders. A large image made of wicker work and filled with combustibles is elevated some seventy feet high. Two beautiful children are drawn in a car richly dressed by two sacred bulls. These children fire two arrows each at the image, and are then taken to the temple, and, as I was informed, sacrificed in the evening amid a great display of fireworks.

All the natives sleep during the great heat of the day, and are up all night around the fires made of horse and cow manure, which keep off mosquitoes. They make a horrid din, beating a drum called *tum, tum,* and singing, so that with the noise all through the bazaars, the drumming and the mosquito chorus, a foreigner has little rest. Our men enjoyed plenty of shooting, sand-geese, ducks, parrots, and peacocks; although dangerous to shoot the latter, the Hindoos holding them as sacred. We had almost everything to beguile our time; drill and field-days at early morning, besides a good library, ball-alley, racket, quoits, cricket, and a theatre, named the Victoria.

Returning to quarters one evening, after a shooting excursion, and the day having been intensely hot, many were enjoying a cool nap on the cot outside the door of the camp. Apart from all the rest, by himself, was an old crusty sergeant, nicknamed "Old Nick,"—a bath, there being plenty about for the use of the men, stood near him, and after a moment's consultation, as he snored away, we decided to play him a trick.

Our party being all of the same rank, (four sergeants) even if we were discovered, it would not be deemed so bad as if it were done by inferiors, but this we thought nothing of. Lifting him very carefully, and so gently as not to disturb his heavy snoring, we conveyed our friend "Old Nick" to the bath, laid him evenly and gently as possible, looking round seeing each our way clear for a good run—let go, and souse he fell into the water. Splutter, splutter, occasionally as we ran, a fierce yell and a curse. We were in bed in five minutes, in fact before he had time to properly shake himself, and although enquiry and enquiry was made, and a reward for the miscreants offered by himself, no one ever learned who did it for years after.

We were not to remain long at peace, war broke out again on the death of Shah Soojah. Akbar Khan had seized the reins of government of Afghanistan, shot Mr. McNaughton, the agent, had prevailed on General Elphinstone to retire, who was weak enough to do so, instead of holding his position until aid arrived; and as soon as Akbar got him into the Guddulock Pass, commenced an indiscriminate, massacre. The 44th Regiment was almost cut to pieces; some were taken prisoners with the officers' wives, including Lady Sale; some few escaped to Jellalabad, at the entrance of the Khyber Pass, where General Sale, Colonel Denny, and Major Havelock were with the 13th Light Infantry. When the winter was far enough advanced to march, Akbar wanted to attack Sale, but he, not wishing to be caught, marched out and met him in battle, and fully routed him and his army. Poor Colonel Denny being killed, Havelock then assumed the command.

In the early spring General Pollock was pushed on with a force from Bengal.

Before I proceed farther I will here give the following incident which occurred at the time of the massacre in the Guddulock Pass, in 1842:—

When the slaughter was nearly complete, a Doctor Brydon endeavoured to escape; among the survivors was a native assistant, who, seeing Brydon sorely pressed, called to him, saying, "Doctor Saib, I cannot possibly escape, I am dying of cold and hunger, take my pony and do the best you can for yourself." Brydon tried to encourage him, but no, he was dying, Brydon mounted, and through the confusion, forced his way to the front. Reaching all safe, he found a group of mounted officers, who knowing they were just at the end of the Pass where it opens on the plain where Jellalabad stands, determined to make a bold push for life. Seeing Brydon on a wretched pony, they declared they could not wait for him, mounted as he was, and any delay would be sure to cause their immediate destruction. On they went, leaving Brydon slowly toiling after them. The Afghans saw the group advancing at full swing, met them and slew them every man, and thinking no one else was coming, went back to the hills; just then Brydon jogged past unobserved.

News of Elphinstone's force was anxiously waited for at Jellalabad. Towards evening one man slowly riding a worn-out pony was descried at the entrance of the Pass,—cavalry were immediately sent to bring him in—it was Brydon. As he entered the gate he fell senseless from fatigue. When restoratives were applied, at least such as were at hand, he revived, and the first question he asked was about his pony, the pony that had saved his life—it was dead. Brydon was with General Sale during the gallant defence of Jellalabad, and lived to take part in the defence of Lucknow.

Pollack pushed through the Khyber Pass to the relief of Sale. Another force under General Nott marched from Bombay towards Ghuznee, to the relief of our troops hemmed in there—the two divisions were to meet at Cabul as an avenging army. Both pushed on as rapidly as possible, and after long and arduous marches, reached Cabul, rescued the prisoners, and burnt the capital to the ground. General Elphinstone having died, completely broken down through this sad disaster. Lord Auckland was called home, and Lord Ellenborough replaced him as Governor-General of India.

In January, 1843, an army of observation was formed on the banks of the Sutlej, to meet Generals Nott and Pollock on their return through the Khyber Pass, bringing with them the gates of the temple of Somnuth, from in front the Mahomedan mosque, at Ghuznee,—carried off eight hundred years before, on the conquest of India and subjugation of the Hindoos—and now restored after that lapse of time by British valour, and thereby conciliating the original possessors of Hindostan.

These gates were made of sandal-wood, each one drawn on a waggon by twelve bullocks; they were also covered with crimson curtains fringed with gold.

The Maharajah of Lahore came down with six thousand cavalry as an escort to pay his respects to Lord Ellenborough. We marched towards Delhi on the first of February, through the protected Sikh states. Arriving at Delhi we encamped on the race course. Lord Ellenborough had summoned all the *rajahs* and petty princes to meet him and the king at a *durbar*, along with the King of Delhi was the Rajah of Burtpoor, the Rajah of Jypoor, the Rajah of Puttealea. All the Indian nobility gave a grand dinner to the Governor-General, Lord Gough, and all the British officers.

A large place was built of wicker-work, covered with flags, banners, streamers, and variegated lamps; and tables were laid for five hundred guests; the service was of silver and gold. The governor-general and staff went down in three carriages, escorted by two troops 16th Lancers—my troop happened to be one of them—when the cavalcade arrived, a royal salute was fired, and salvo after salvo almost shook the air; the crowd was so dense we could almost ride over turbaned heads. After dinner there was a grand presentation to Lord Ellenborough,—a gold salver full of jewels, two elephants, richly caparisoned, and four Arab horses—then came such a display of fireworks as never has been equalled since. It was twelve p.m. before we started for camp.

The day following all this display a grand field-day was held, in order to show these native princes the power of Britain, and what good soldiers she boasted of. In all the movements, the troops sustained their traditional name; the 16th made a dashing charge, covering the infantry, who had fallen into square; we astonished the king and the several princes by the quickness of our movements, they calling us the *Lall Goral Wallas*, or *Bullam Wallas*. We broke up in a few days afterwards, each regiment marching to their respective stations, the 16th back to Meerut, where we arrived on the 4th of March.

I might have introduced to the reader before this an inseparable companion I had while in cantonments, and one who not only shared my bed and board, but one who, during many hours of serious thought and fretfulness about all at home, mother and sisters, made me laugh and forget what I had been thinking about a few moments before; this creature was Jaco, my monkey; where he was born, or where he originally sprung from, or his race, I cannot tell. I am no Darwinian, but positively, the amount of tact and knowledge displayed by Jaco, often since has led me to consider our possible relationship well. I purchased Jaco for a small sum from a native, intending, if he remained with me, to train him well and keep him as a companion; I took him to my quarters, and as a first lesson to teach him subjection and obedience, tied him to the handle of my trunk; here, I kept him sufficiently long, that, by kind treatment, I thought I had weaned him from any bad tricks he had learned; he, of course, got quite used to a sword, a carbine, and of my dress; I made him a nice-fitting scarlet jacket, blue pants, and a cap with gold lace, and, dear me, how I laughed to see my tiny mock soldier strutting about; this pleased him well.

My comrade had a spaniel dog. Jaco and the spaniel got quite friendly. This creature was also very biddable, and on both, my comrade and I commenced a series of drill, providing Jaco with a wooden sword. In a short time they got so advanced, that on the word "mount," Jaco would stride the spaniel, and away out with either of us to parade for guard mounting; this they continued to do, till mounting guard became an everyday's duty, creating a great amount of laughter, and they were never absent. If I happened to be tired, and lying down getting a little rest, Jaco would jump on the table, make faces at himself in the glass, then, to annoy me, or get me up, as he knew he was disturbing me, get pen and ink, as he had seen me do, and destroy any paper that lay about with his scrawling; if I took no notice, and he found it was no use teasing me that way, he usually licked the pen, spitting out several times, make ugly faces, all the time looking at me, I pretending to sleep.

I don't know that he had one bad habit, but thieving, and this he was expert at; if I had received a paper, or was sending one home, and left it on the table, nothing pleased poor Jaco better than to make away with it. His usual plan was to leap on my table, watch me well for a time, to make sure I was asleep, he gently came on the bed, above my head, put his finger softly to my eyes and try to open them; this was done, I suppose, to see if I would stir, then with a bound away on the table, seize the package, and away to the woods, where he generally remained till night, when he quietly came back, getting into bed at my feet.

Jaco was a great pet all over the cantonment. I intended, if I had been fortunate enough in keeping him, to bring him home: he, however, often got me into blame for his thieving tricks, and one day returned to my tent with a broken arm; how he got it I could never make out; I applied splints, and he seemed to recover the use of it, but I fancied the pain drove him mad, for he went to the woods one day, and never came back.

CHAPTER 4

The Queen and
Her Army Surrender

Peace was not of long duration. The old King of Rio Scinde having died, the British Government, by treaty with him, were bound to see his son established on his throne. It was now usurped by the *Rannie* of Gwalior, who deposed the rightful heir.

The 16th Lancers were ordered to join the army summoned to assemble at Agra to meet the governor-general and Lord Gough, on the 15th November. The Cawnpore division, under General Grey, were moving up on the other side. The Meerut division consisted of ourselves—three troops horse artillery, 39th and 40th Regiments, three regiments of native infantry, a battery foot artillery, three companies sappers and miners. We were received by Lord Gough, who lately arrived from England as commander-in-chief, with Sir Harry Smith as adjutant-general, and Colonel Havelock, my old friend, as Persian interpreter.

Agra was at one time the summer residence of the Moghul of Delhi—it stands on the Jumna river, whose waters lave the walls of the Palace. On the marble slab in front of the throne, where in days gone by stood many a proud Mahometan, when the Rajpoots lorded over the conquered Hindoos, stood Lord Ellenborough, representative of proud England, surrounded by her warriors and heroes of many a hard-fought battle, and knighted Generals Pollock and Nott by Her Majesty's command for bravery. In Agra also is the tomb or *targ* of the great and mighty Ackbar's favourite daughter, built of white marble, and looked upon as one of the wonders of the world for its unsurpassing grandeur—it was erected 700 years ago. Under the immense dome are two slabs, covering the mausoleum, inlaid with precious stones. The dome is flanked by four marble minarets 150 feet in height—the garden approaching the tomb is full of orange and lemon trees—the sacred lotus flower perfumes the air—every spot around it is sacred to the Mahometan.

The order to march was issued on the 20th of November. This is the most delightful time of the year in India—not so hot during the day—mornings and evenings lovely and cool. The country of the *ryots* through which we marched is certainly a beautiful one, judging at this time of the year. They are mostly Hindoos, are quiet, harmless and industrious. It looked strange to us, now so near Christmas, to see hundreds of acres of golden wheat ready for harvesting—no hedges or fencing here, but as far as the eye can reach one field of waving yellow, mixed with red poppy.

The Hindoos are firm believers in transmigration, consequently never eat any animal food. The *Brama* or Sacred Bull, mostly white, with a hump on his shoulders, his head hung with garlands of flowers, is allowed to range where he likes, and is fed out of flour or sugar-barrels, and none dare molest him. The women are most degraded—never educated,—they are not supposed to possess souls—they never eat with men, and among the high caste they are not allowed to be seen by another man. After marriage, which is contracted when about twelve years of age, they are old and ugly when thirty is reached. When I have seen a group of these girls waiting with their lamps at the four corners of the road for the bridegroom, I have often thought of the parable of the *Ten Virgins*.

Our march was generally finished by nine in the morning. After guards and pickets have been placed, I have nearly always visited the nearest village, having learned some Hindoostanee. I could make them understand. I always found them civil and kind, but afraid of soldiers, some Europeans being very insulting, and even I have heard complaints of being robbed of fruit, poultry, or anything suitable to them. The followers of an Indian army being all natives, but of course of different parts of India, are generally great thieves. Naturally an army *en route* is very destructive, so many animals to feed—elephants, camels, horses. The Government profess to pay for everything used, especially if camped in a grain or cotton field.

We arrived at the River Chumble on 24th December, and moved as follows:—16th Lancers in front, 40th following, up to their armpits in water, next the artillery, then the 39th, and so on. We had information before crossing that the enemy would probably oppose the landing, as they were in the neighbour-hood, but we saw none of them. We were ordered to gallop to the front and reconnoitre. As we advanced about five miles we saw the enemy's camp at a distance between two villages. We halted allowing the column to come up. The ground here was very rough, and interspersed by ugly ravines.

Between us and them was a very deep *nulla*, with only two places to ford it, five miles apart. Wet as we were from our recent fording the Chumla, I had to go on in charge of the advance guard and remain all night. Our baggage, or tents, not having come up—what was worse the commissariat had not arrived, and we felt hungry. The enemy's cavalry were reconnoitering on our front, and during the night a very strict watch was kept up. Morning at last dawned, beautiful as weather could make it—Christmas morning and all—and a pretty plight it found us in, hungry, wet clothes, and if we wanted to drink we had plenty muddy water.

About four o'clock, p. m., I was ordered to mount again, take twenty men, and strengthen the outlying pickets. We had not taken off boots or clothes for four days, nor had the saddles been off the horses during the same time. I was further directed by the officer in charge of the picket, after I had reported to him, to take six troopers to the front as an extra lookout on the ford, patrolling myself between my post and the main picket every half-hour. About twelve at night a rocket went up from a village within our lines, and was answered immediately by a light from the enemy's camp. The village was at once surrounded, and every man in it made prisoners. I suffered fearfully that night, being so long in the saddle with wet trousers; my legs were as raw as a piece of beef. Give me fighting—fair open fighting, at once—in preference to such torture. We waited here, without attacking, three days, expecting some of General Grey's division, mainly from Cawnpore, towards Gwalior.

On the night of the 28th we got orders quietly to turn out at 4 o'clock in the morning, 29th December, to march without baggage or other incumbrance, with one day's cooked rations. We fell into line exactly to time, when Lord Gough with Lord Ellenborough and staff rode along the front, speaking words of encouragement to each corps.

Sir Joseph Thackwell, who had only one arm, commanded the Light Division, consisting of the 16th Lancers, Body Guards, three troops Horse Artillery, Outram's Irregulars. The centre division was commanded by Colonel Vallient, comprised the 40th Foot, two batteries foot artillery, two corps of native infantry, one company of engineers. The left division consisting of 39th Foot, five native cavalry, two regiments native infantry, and one company of sappers under Sir Harry Smith. Each division crossed the ravine within one mile of each other. They were in position between three villages—Maharajpoor in the centre, Juna on the right, and Chuna on the left. We marched until seven o'clock, when we halted. The enemy at once opened fire from their half-moon battery. Nothing could be more welcome; we hurrahed several times and shouted lustily, "There goes the Prize-Money," showing, without doubt, the general feeling of our army,—there was no such thing as failure.

The trumpeter now sounded for us "To Horse, To Horse," and away we went at a swinging trot to the front, preceded by Quarter-Master General Churchill, as it is that officer's business to learn the position of an enemy, and the nature of the ground, we advanced in close column of troops. Our route lay through a cotton plantation, and on nearing the enemy we were received by a discharge from a six-gun battery. A six-pound shot took my horse in the heart, and we both rolled over. I was extricated by some grenadiers of a native regiment just passing, much bruised.

I was not long without a horse, as peppering had been going on by the advanced picket, a horse, minus the rider, fully accoutred, which had belonged to the enemy, passed. I seized it, and soon came up with my troop. We formed in line, in front of us being a field of wheat standing in shocks; these we found occupied by the enemy's sharpshooters, quite concealed.

A shot from one of these picked off General Churchill; as he fell, Colonel Somerset, an *aide*, dismounted to assist him; he was nearly as unfortunate, as a shot from one of their batteries broke his leg, killing his horse on the spot—poor Churchill died as he was being taken to the rear. The battle now became more fierce. The centre division, led by the 40th, under Colonel Vallient, charged, and at the point of the bayonet took the village of Maharajpoor. Just then, the enemy's cavalry were coming down like a dark cloud upon our guns, when the 16th, my regiment, and the Body Guards were ordered to charge; this we were quite prepared to do, as soldiers, at least so far as my experience teaches, do not like to be onviewers, or watchers.

Charge we did, but to our astonishment, as soon as they saw our movement, retreat was their order, and we afterwards heard they never stopped until they reached Gwalior. At noon the battle was over, the enemy fled, leaving all their camp equipage, guns, and about six thousand dead on the field. Their force was estimated 24,000, while ours only numbered 10,000, in having left 4,000 to protect our camp and hospital. Our loss was 2,500 officers, rank and file.

The following day we pushed on, halting some fifteen miles from Gwalior. Here we camped for a time. The *rannee*, or queen, came down with a strong guard, four thousand cavalry, to pay her respects, and make terms of peace with Lord Ellenborough. He would not hear of any only an unconditional surrender. The day after the *rannee's* visit we marched on the capital, reaching Gwalior about nine a.m. Of all the fortified places ever I had seen, this was the most formidable. A large rock in the centre of an extensive plain, the city built in the middle, and so surrounded by the rocky wall, as to leave only one ascent, and that a zigzag one. The walls all round were loop-holed and bristled with cannon. Our first thought was—We are done now. But, of course, engineering skill and brave hearts laugh at stone walls. All was got ready to storm, as if taken, it must be taken at a dash, and as is always the case, a flag of truce was despatched to warn of our intention of giving them one hour to choose between unconditional surrender or the consequence of a refusal. In half that time the *ranee* and her army marched out, a battalion of our infantry entered, and hoisted the British flag on the walls.

We remained in Gwalior until joined by General Grey on January 3rd. This division had marched from Cawnpore, and consisted of the 9th Lancers, 3rd Buff's, three regiments native infantry, two brigades of artillery, and the 50th Foot, under command of Colonel Anderson. They had been engaged with other portions of the enemy at Punneah on the same day we were fighting at Maharajpoor.

On the 4th, the day following, the entire army was paraded to do honour to the young king, who had been reinstated on his throne, the ceremony being performed before all the people, in front of the city—and oh the following day we were reviewed by Lord Gough, in presence of His Majesty, Lord Ellenborough, and the king's ministers. In the governor-general's address of thanks to the army, he promised us a medal in shape of a star for the capture of Gwalior, and the *ranee*, though now deposed, gave one *crore* of rupees. This was given directly, and a squadron of the 9th and one of the 16th Lancers escorted it in bags, carried by fourteen camels, to the commander-in-chief's camp.

In any part of India I have ever been, I have always seen plenty of game, but the territory of Gwalior can certainly boast of more than any other. The gardens were laid out beautiful. Fruit of every kind was abundant. The principal people here are half Portuguese.

The following incident occurred on one of my shooting excursions. Three of us went out looking for pea-fowl, as they make a beautiful dish. We reached a Mango grove, and sat under a tree. A stream of water ran a few yards away from us, beautiful in appearance to bathe in. Robert Prichard, a corporal in the regiment, one of us, took it into his head to bathe. I remonstrated with him, urging probably the presence of venomous snakes or serpents, very numerous in the Bengal Presidency. He would go, and go he did. My last words were: "Bob, don't you go."

As he started, immediately there came the same words— "Bob, don't you go"—"Bob, don't you go," again came more rapidly. Bob did turn back rather afraid, still he persuaded himself he was no coward, away he went again, and again the same words came thick and fast, "Bob, don't you go," "Bob, don't you go." On looking up we discovered a number of brown birds, similar in appearance to thrushes, in the trees, and as we rose to leave the cry went on, "Bob, don't you go," "Bob, don't you go," but Bob did bathe, and was bitten by a venomous snake, and died that evening.

I have previously stated that the Hindoos are very superstitious, and do not kill anything—not even the poisonous snake. This part of India is not much travelled over by Europeans, and all sorts of dangerous reptiles and wild beasts live on undisturbed to kill man.

The 16th Lancers had by this time completed twenty-two years' service in India, and naturally enough, many looked forward for the order to bring them back to England. It was not to be yet, however, although we all thought that the 9th had come out to relieve us.

On the third of February we broke up camp, and commenced and marched back to our several cantonments. On our way the time passed pleasantly enough. After camp-pitching for the day, if a village was within easy distance, I generally went thither, accompanied by some companion. Generally the villagers will shy away when they get a glimpse of a soldier, they are afraid of being plundered, but the most reasonable excuse is, I think, to be found in their religion being insulted, at least here, for almost everything is sacred. Their former rulers, the *rajahs*, plundered unmercifully, and allowed their men to commit the vilest of crimes.

So full is this country of game as we neared the River Chumble, where I had on my way up got such a severe wetting in crossing, as to fasten a severe cold on me for some days. One morning at sunrise, geese, duck, and other water-fowl rose off the water in such a large dense cloud as to darken the air, as if a thunder-storm were coming on. No one with us ever saw such a multitude. Like every other living thing, they are never disturbed, but live on and multiply.

No matter what our position in life—either high or low—or whatever our tastes for a variety of food, no men feel the loss of satisfying this desire more than soldiers on a campaign, always confined to the same diet. I have heard old soldiers say they remembered they had such an abhorrence for hard biscuit, and such an appetite for fresh bread, impossible to get at the time, that if a year's pay could get one fresh loaf, they would give it. We felt now something of this feeling, and all ranks longed for a change of some sort, either in bread or meat. Here was a fine opportunity, and it was availed of to the full extent, as far as the animal food could do it.

Three of our officers. Captain Meek, Lieutenant Patterson, and the Veterinary Surgeon, respectively nicknamed—Meek, The Hair Trunk; Patterson, Black Jack; and the veterinary, Hotwater Jack were sitting together engaged in mending their jackets and pants, one occasionally rising to feed the fire over which was pinioned on the sticks a leg of a stag or of mutton, I could not say which, and no doubt, as they felt hungry, anticipating a nice feed, when all of a sudden we were startled by shouts and hurrahs and roars of laughter. A dog had stolen unawares, when they were engaged in their tailoring, and making one bounce, seized the roasting limb, and away with him. The three, with jackets pants and flannels flying from their arms, after the poor hungry brute, shouting with all their might— "Stop thief! stop thief!" It was relished after all, notwithstanding the extra handling and dog-bites it got.

After passing the river and ascending the hill on the opposite bank, we came suddenly on a herd of antelopes. So astonished did they seem, on perceiving horsemen, they actually stood staring at us, until nearing them, they started at a bound, some dashing through the ranks of our squadron. One of our men gave chase to a splendid buck, as he ran towards a village, near which we knew was a pond. The stag took to it; the man followed, having jumped off his horse, and seized him by the horns. The stag was the strongest, and dashed the man away in the water; still he held on until an officer coming on the scene, stabbed him, and, amid roars of laughter, the corporal emerged, covered with green slime and chickweed. That day we had venison for twelve, the officers taking the rest.

Agra and Delhi was at last reached, then Meerut on the 4th March, having been five months on that campaign, and lost fifty men from the regiment. Here we passed the hot season, from the middle of March to the beginning of May, as what are called the hot winds blow from eight in the morning till between four and five in the evening, no one in that time can stir out of doors— not even the natives can stand the scorching heat. The torment, the mosquitoes, are busy humming all this time. I have seen men almost blinded with their swollen faces; however, there is one relief, every soldier can have a native to fan him, and keep them off. Another pest during this season is found in the numbers of jackals who run in packs at night, and actually bold enough to get under the beds.

CHAPTER 5

Ordered to Punjaub

Old companionship of regiment is never forgotten in the service. We had beside us now in cantonment the Fortieth Foot, a corps that had served in times gone by with the 16th in the Peninsular wars and at Waterloo. They had now been four years in Afghanistan, were present at Kilat, Gilzie and Candahar. Having plenty of money on hand, after our late campaign, we often fraternized with them, and indeed were boon companions as far as we could in the pleasures and enjoyments of camp life at Meerut. Dinners and parties, at which I am sorry to add much intoxication prevailed, was an everyday occurrence. So much was revelling carried on that on General Arbuthnot coming to the station to assume command, and when at dinner with the colonel, the state of the regiment was the subject of discussion. This was the question, "What would you do, Colonel, if your regiment was required tomorrow morning for immediate service; they are all drunk and wandering about anywhere."

This matter was soon settled by a heavy wager—I suppose merely in name—by the colonel, who stated the regiment would be out at daylight in the morning—it was then ten o'clock—and if any man was absent, or should fall off his horse, the bet was forfeited. The Adjutant, Lieutenant Dynon, gave orders at once to sound "boot and saddle," the regiment to turn out half-an-hour before daylight. The trumpeters did their duty, galloped all over the lines sounding the alarm; the men tumbled in from all directions.

The hour named for the parade arrived—the regiment, complete, not a man absent, stood out on the plain awaiting the general and his staff. They, accompanied by a number of ladies, put in an appearance. The roll was called in front of them, and with the exception of ninety-seven men, invalids in hospital, every man of the corps was present. To test the regiment more thoroughly, twenty-four difficult movements were gone through at a gallop, then we advanced in review order, every horse covered with foam. The general, of course, could do nothing after losing his wager, and witnessing our splendid movements, but compliment us most highly. As we marched back to cantonments we were wildly cheered by native and European regiments, and as a reward we received from the colonel a few more days' leave for enjoyment. Dinner parties and suppers commenced again, and continued well up to the time the Fortieth were ordered to Calcutta, to embark for England

In July the rainy season commences. It falls in torrents three weeks at a time, forming deep *nullas* or ravines, which make it difficult, indeed dangerous, to get about, and this lasts till after the middle of August.

In November, the Ninth Lancers came up from Cawnpore, and as we had not met them, or at least the two regiments had not been together since eighteen hundred and eighteen, what could be expected than that another fraternization as had taken place with the Fortieth would be repeated. This I need hardly say occurred, and continued till the 9th marched for Umballa.

We now enter the months when fruit and vegetables get ripe, and many a visit we had from the natives to our camp, driving or rather leading their *tattoos* on ponies laden with luxurious fruit. The mango is here very plentiful, and it may be interesting to describe it, the most delicious fruit in the world. The tree is about the size of a large oak; the fruit, when ripe, is of a greenish yellow, with reddish cheeks, the skin, when removed, presents a sort of jelly; a small stone, the size of a peach stone, in the middle. "We eat them out of a large pan, in which is first placed some cold water. We had also plentiful supplies of guava, custard fruit, plantain, banana, and water-melon of the size of an English beer-barrel for three *pice*, or a penny.

Some five miles from Meerut cantonments is a town called Sedanna, where the *begum* or queen resided, who was once the monarch of this district, subject only to the once powerful Mogul of Delhi, but at this time a pensioner of the East India Company. There is a curious story told of this extraordinary woman, and I will here give it. She was the favourite of a *rajah* who reigned some years back. She was instrumental in raising a revolt, and then urged him to fly, which he did. She, of course, accompanied him, but carried in a *palanquin*. While in this conveyance she pretended to stab herself, and screamed wildly. When the *rajah* heard it, thinking she had been assassinated—not a very uncommon thing in India—he plunged a *poniard* into his heart, and died on the spot.

No sooner was the *rajah* dead than she jumped on a horse, galloped back, surrounded by her guards, collected the army, harangued them, saying she would now lead them to victory. They cheered. She did lead them against a powerful enemy, and by her perseverance—a second Joan of Arc—conquered. She was established in the favour of her army, who confirmed her queen. Subsequently she married a French adventurer, Sombra Dyce, and made him general. He, being a Roman Catholic, converted her, at least nominally, built a chapel, which I have been in, and in which she had a tomb erected to the memory of the old *rajah*, her first husband. There is also another to that of Sombra Dyce, her second. She had two sons by her second marriage, who were always at law with the old East India Company, claiming some possessions of their mother; but I could never learn the result, as the appeals were frequent to the Home Government.

She was now getting old, but frequently came to our cantonment, as she was friendly with our colonel, and loved to see the 16th Lancers. She has even been to our theatre, and whenever, in passing, she saw any children, always threw them handfuls of silver coin. A number of her people had embraced Christianity, who were ministered to by a regular priest. Whenever we strolled out to her palace we were received very kindly, were allowed the use of her billiard tables, as all the furniture was of European make, and many a good picnic we enjoyed in the mango grove of the palace.

On Sunday, the thirteenth November, 1845, as we were marching from church, news soon spread that war had again broken out, and the Meerut division were to make forced marches to join Lord Gough, who had pushed on from Umballa, as the Sikhs had crossed into our territory in large force near Ferozepoor. The Cawnpore and Delhi divisions were also to move lip in haste. This was astounding news to men so long in India as most of the 16th had been, but nevertheless all felt glad—in fact rejoiced—at the prospects of another good campaign, so eager were our men for it that the sick in hospital, such as were convalescent, would persuade the surgeon they were well enough, and begged to be let go with the regiment.

Before starting, we had learned a civil war had broken out in the Punjaub. The *rannee* had dethroned Dulep Sing, the rightful heir, the army was divided—one half for her, and the other against—and this state of things had been going on for several months; we then, the army of Her Majesty, as is always the case, had to set matters right. Before entering upon any further particulars, a short history of the Sing family will not be out of place.

Runjeit Sing was the founder of the dynasty; he was a powerful chief, having conquered all the smaller chiefs around him, established himself as *maharajah* at Lahore. In time, two French officers came along from Persia, soldiers of fortune, as such men are to be found everywhere, ready for anything as long as they get good pay. These men had served under the first Napoleon. One of them offered to raise a regiment to imitate the old French Imperial Guards, and the other made similar offers to raise one of cavalry. The offer was accepted. Both regiments were risen to the satisfaction of the *rajah*; he made the first a general, the second a colonel. To one, the general, he gave one of his daughters to wife. Subsequently, another Frenchman came into the county, named La Court, and his services were accepted, so that between the three old French soldiers the *rajah* raised a powerful and well-equipped force; and having defeated a powerful neighbouring chief at Rungier, or the seven-hilled city, he became master of the whole Punjaub, or country of five rivers.

After these successes he attacked the Afghans, drove them out of Pesheva, and took possession of the entrance of the Khyber, where he built the fort alluded to previously in this work, called Junrood. Runjeit Sing signifies, in their language, Fierce Lion. When he succeeded thus far in his conquests it became apparent he had an eye on Bengal, and thought he could drive the British back to the sea. His French generals, however, told him different, advising him not to interfere with them, or he might lose all. Craftiness, and perhaps fear, caused him to become an ally, as he made a treaty with Lord Auckland, signing it on the banks of the Sutlej river, bringing very valuable presents to be sent to our Queen. Four sons survived him, named Currick Sing, Nunihall Sing, Sheer Sing, and Dulep Sing. The first three were easily made away with by assassination, by the favourite Queen, who had the youngest, Dulep, placed in the harem, where old Runjeit had five hundred wives and concubines. Having accomplished all this, she united the contending parties under her paramour, Lai Sing, meditating an attack upon the East India Company territories. They assembled at the fort of Umritsa seventy thousand strong, crossed the Sutlej before our Government were aware of their doings.

Their first action was with Lord Gough, at Mudkee, 19th December, 1845, where he was encamped. The men, when surprised, were preparing their morning meal; they soon, however, got in fighting trim, some in their shirt-sleeves. The 3rd Light Dragoons, assisted by the fiftieth foot and others, gained a complete victory over them. It was here General Sir R. Sale got killed. Lord Gough pushed on that night, 21st December, and came on the main body encamped at Ferosha, fought them all that day, 22nd, and but for a ruse would have been surely defeated. Ammunition falling short, a troop of Horse Artillery galloped off to Ferospoor for a supply.

The enemy's cavalry, seeing them through a cloud of sand, imagined their retreat was being cut off, panic-stricken, they bolted, when the 3rd Light Dragoons and 4th Native Cavalry charged under a heavy fusillade from the infantry—50th and

62nd—completely routed them from their position. In this charge. Colonel Somerset, aide to Lord Gough, was killed. The Meerut division knew nothing of all this until we arrived at Mudkee on the 1st January, when the sights we met confirmed our suspicion. At first we came across dead camels, then, on approaching the village, several of our native regiment soldiers came out to greet us. A sad sight indeed—some bandaged almost from head to foot; arms and legs off. All left behind in the hurry to keep up with the enemy.

On laying out our picket guard with the quarter-master general, as I was in the advanced guard, we came upon a heap of sand, out of which part of a man's hand projected; also, a little further on, part of a hand and wrist, with so much of the cuff of a coat as showed a 50th button. We, of course, performed the duty of burying all such, as the pursuing army had no time. Making a reconnaissance with my captain, we entered a kind of park-like enclosure, and here we found traces of the fearful work of Gough's engagement. Men, horses, and camels lay in heaps unburied, vultures in hundreds feasting on them; none had been touched, all lay as they fell. The Sikhs lay in heaps under their guns, the Light Dragoons as they fell from their horses, the tents of the blind half-hundred still standing, knapsacks around in all directions. The guns we secured, and fatigue parties performed the sickening duty of burying the dead.

CHAPTER 6

Battle of Aliwal Commenced

After this melancholy duty was performed, we pushed on to the Sutlej River, to overtake Lord Gough, and on the 5th January reached Hureka Gaut, encamping on the right of his lordship's division. We lay here till the 15th, when General Sir Harry Smith was ordered to intercept Rungour Sing, he having crossed the river higher up, and burnt Loodianna, one of our stations. On the third day's march Sir Harry sent back for reinforcements, and the 16th Lancers, with a troop of artillery, was sent to him. We made forced marches in order to overtake him, which we did at Jugram; here we were joined by the 77th, having been pushed up from Calcutta. On the evening of the 20th we received orders to leave all our tents and baggage; subsequently the order to take all was given, and we mounted at 3 o'clock next morning, stopping at eight to roll our cloaks. As we were doing so, some of the lookout descried the enemy's cavalry. We remounted, and, as usual, I was sent on the advance picket.

A large body of cavalrymen were moving in front, parallel with us. Soon we made a sand-hill, and on going up it saw the Fort heavily mounted with cannon, thousands of bayonets glittering in the morning sun. This was Buddiwal, a village lying between us and it. We halted till the body of the regiment came up, when a battery opened on us. The 31st Foot behind could scarcely travel up—the sand was so deep. Sir Harry rode to our colonel, telling him to keep ground with the artillery till all the infantry had passed on, as he did not intend to fight them that day, but would pass on to Loodianna, They were 20,000 strong,

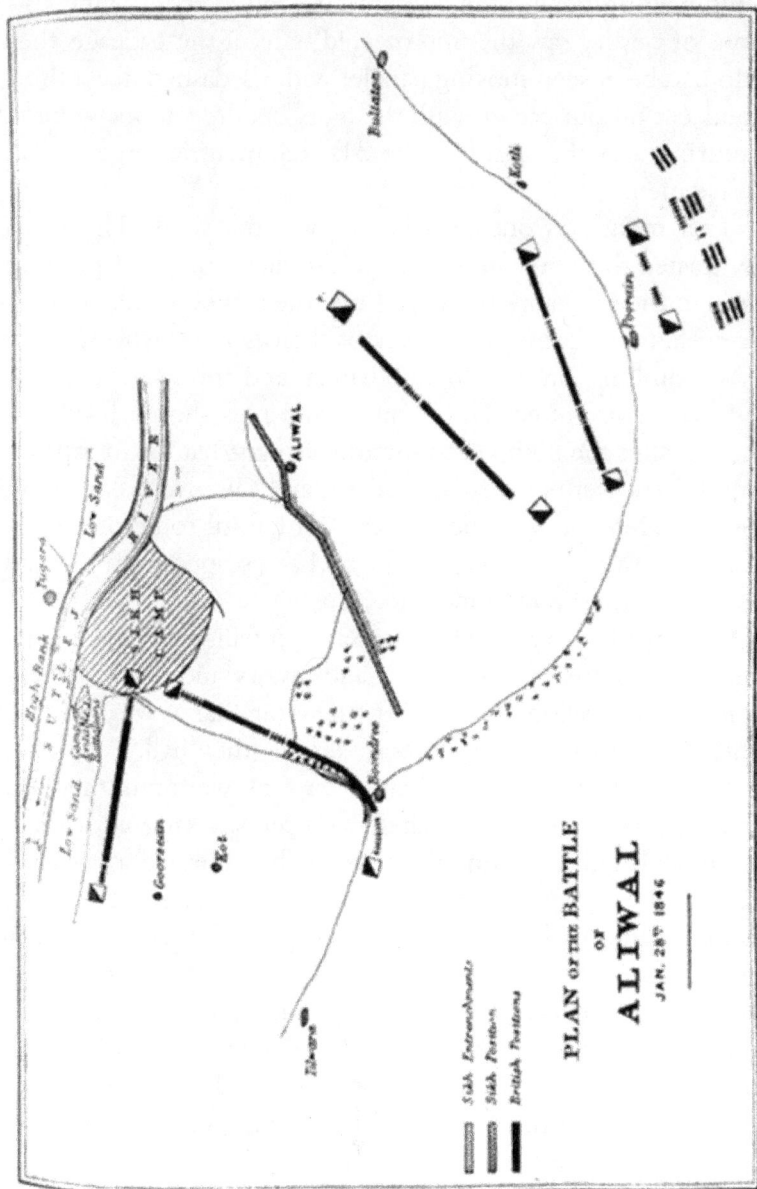

PLAN OF BATTLE OF ALIWAL

we only about 4,000. Here was evidently some error, or some order neglected, for the baggage was too far in rear instead of being well up behind the column. As soon as these flying columns of cavalry saw the unprotected state of the baggage, they who had been seen moving parallel with us, dashed like a thick cloud, cut off our camels with the tents, bedding, money-chests, capturing also the guard of the 31st regiment, a sergeant and twelve men.

That night was one of debauch over the spoils. They cruelly treated their prisoners. The Sikh soldiers run a red-hot iron through the sergeant's body. This treatment they would all have received, but it came to the ears of their general who stopped it. We, pushing on, got to Loodianna, and found great havoc had been committed. The barracks and mess-house had been burned, after the 50th left to join the army. What few troops we found there were our native soldiers, and they were shut up in the fort. Here we remained till the 23rd, until some of our elephants with tents and baggage, who had escaped from the raid and gone a long way round, came up.

On 23rd January, Sir Harry received intelligence; the enemy were in full retreat from the fort, and cavalry and horse artillery went off at a gallop to intercept them. Sir Harry was too late; when we got to the fort it was deserted—they had the start of us. Ordered to dismount and enter the fort, we found they had burnt the bedding, money-chests and tents, taking with them all of value, and it was quite apparent they hurried away, fearing we would come down on them from Loodianna. The town also bore the marks everywhere of a quick departure. On entering the palace, we found it undisturbed, profusely furnished with European furniture; and on going into one of the best rooms, my comrade and I heard some women scream. Rushing to where the sound proceeded from— an adjacent room—we saw some of our native cavalry ill-treating two women—Circassians—who had belonged to the *rajah's* harem. They were forcing their jewellery off them.

On seeing two white soldiers, they ran to us. By persuasion, and at times by threats, they showed us where some money was hid. Taking us into the Seraglio, they pointed out a black stone near a fire stove. The floor of this apartment was made of marble, chequered black and white. On lifting the stone pointed out, we discovered two bags containing *rupees*. Counting them in camp, one had three hundred, the other four hundred and fifty. The girls were beautiful Circassian slaves, and could not have cost less than one thousand *rupees* each. They were much obliged to us, saying, "Company Dewoy, thank you, thank you." We had great fun that night in camp, appropriating anything found of use. We killed cows and sheep, made cakes, had plenty of milk, and, besides, the two young Circassians attended on us.

Reinforcements of infantry constantly arriving from Lord Gough, on the 26th we numbered 10,000 fighting men, and on the 28th we were to march to meet the enemy, who had recrossed the Sutlej, and added to their number 4,000 men, making them 24,000 in all. We marched in solid square; cavalry in front, then infantry, artillery in centre, and cavalry in rear. The enemy were in sight, as reported by our advance picket, at eight o'clock. As we got near, they moved out of camp, and deployed into line. The 16th Lancers, with the 5th Native Cavalry and two troops of horse artillery, were ordered to the left. Two regiments of native cavalry, with horse artillery and 31st and 50th Foot in centre, all flanked by four regiments of native infantry.

The enemy commenced the action at half- past eight, opening a heavy cannonade from the village of Aliwal, their centre—their line reaching three miles from right to left. Very soon the 31st and 50th stormed the village. Colonel Cureton, of the 16th, Brigadier of Cavalry, turned the enemy's left by a rapid movement of cavalry and artillery. On the right a large body of choice Sikh troops were coming down through a wood to outflank us. On this being apparent, our left wing—the 16th Lancers and the 5th Native Cavalry—charged, putting them to the route. I was acting as orderly to Sir Harry, and just where we stood a shell from the enemy, as it flew above us, burst overhead, a piece falling and cutting his telescope in two, as he took it from his eye. This seemingly vexed Sir Harry, for he immediately despatched me to Major Smyth, commanding the right wing, with orders

Major Smyth

to take that battery.

As I delivered the order I fell in with my troop. In front was a battalion of the *rajah's* Guards in square. Major Smyth shouted, "Boys, three cheers for the Queen."— "Lancers charge." Away we went as fast as horses could gallop, right through the square, and away to the battery of guns, sabering the gunners, and captured and spiked the guns. An incident is here worthy of recording. The square was just broken by a corporal named Newsome, leaping his horse right into it. As he jumped he shouted, "Here goes, boys; death or a commission!" Unfortunately for the country, and the service, to which he was an ornament, he was killed, and when found, after the square was broken, he had nineteen bayonet stabs on his body, with the green standard of Mahomet in the grasp of his hand. My lieutenant was wounded, and the cornet killed here, the sergeant-major severely wounded. We were separated from the wing. I gave the word "about," and as we came back, it was as bad as going to the front. The enemy were scattered, firing in every direction. Our major fell from his horse wounded. Him we brought to the rear, when we met the general, who shouted: "Well done 16th, you have immortalized yourselves today." Missing so many officers, he added: "Where are your officers—all wounded or dead?"

On being informed, he desired me to take the remnant of the troop and join the squadron going over the hill there, pointing them out. I had 45 men out of 87. We joined the other squadron just in time; it was commanded by Major Beer, and was just about charging another square, enfiladed by artillery; having done so, a retreat of the whole enemy was the result. We followed in pursuit to the river; our guns cut their bridge of boats; the flying enemy took to the water—and such a sight!—men, horses, camels, artillery all swamping together. Our gunners, in addition, shelling them from the shores. This was the last of glorious Aliwal.

We formed on the bank, cavalry and artillery. Sir Harry passed along our front as we gave a ringing cheer, his hat in hand. "Men," said he, "it is I should cheer you, for you did the work. Your Queen and country shall know of it." Then another

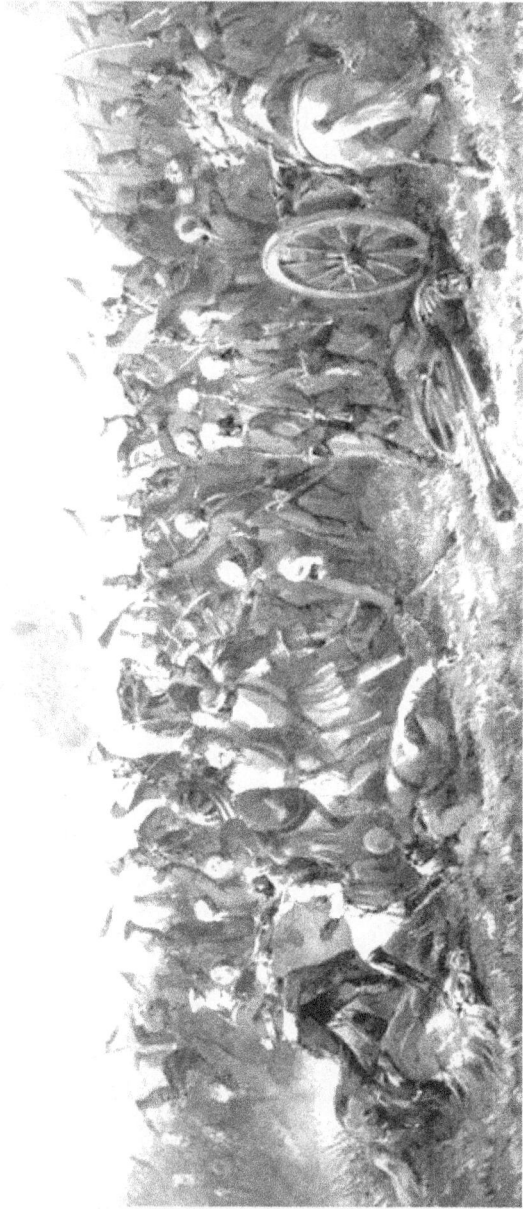

Battle of Aliwal

ringer. And now for the melancholy part of the work. We had not tasted meet or drink since six o'clock in the morning; it was now evening, We had five miles to go over to collect the wounded, and bury the dead. The carnage was fearful; horses, dead and mutilated most fearfully, as they plunge very much when wounded. Several were trying to get about on three legs; we killed these outright. Where the fighting was close, as in square, men's bodies were thickest; wounded in all conceivable ways; jaws shot away; often heads; some disembowelled.

But enough—it is not pleasant to remember, particularly some who were near comrades; we lost in all seventy-six officers and men killed, seventy-seven wounded, and one hundred and sixty horses. Five thousand of the enemy had been killed, besides a number drowned in the river on the retreat. We captured fifty pieces of artillery and all their camp. It was laughable to see a man of the 31st lugging to his camp an elephant, by a piece of rope tied to his trunk, and another with three camels tied together. In the evening I was ordered to take some wounded to the hospital at the village, two miles back. On getting there, the wounded were laid out on straw down the centre street, the surgeons busy in their shirt sleeves amputating arms and legs by the light of torches.

Riding back in the dark we could plainly hear the groans of the wounded and dying Sikhs; we could not help them, and even if we attempted, they have been known, even when almost dead, stretching out their hand and stabbing a *sepoy* or one of our own, who may have been near them. However, all of ours were collected; when we got back the army was preparing to bivouac for the night on the field. The following day was spent in preparing lists of wounded and killed, and seeing the former as comfortable as possible under cover of tents. On the 30th the wounded and the guns captured were sent to Loodianna.

During the charge of the 16th Lancers through the squares of the Imperial Guards, a sergeant of my troop received a musket shot in the left side, and his horse also was shot dead. Then he was attacked by four Sikhs; he defended himself bravely with his sword, having cut down three. The fourth was about to finish him when a little *ghoorka* at a distance levelled his rifle and shot the foe, thus saving the sergeant. Yet he died a few days after.

These *Ghoorkas* are small hill-tribe men. Under the Company there are three battalions, officered by British officers, and good soldiers they are, loyal and brave. They carry three formidable knives in the shape of a sickle, and they have been known to kill a bear or tiger single-handed. They are recruited from the tribes in the Himalaya Mountains beyond Simla and Nina Tal. The officers and merchants, who reside on the hills during the hot season, keep a number of these small hill men as servants to carry the *jampam*, or fetch wood and water, each family dressing them in Highland costume. They are very honest and industrious. Numbers of them come in from the valleys with walnuts and other fruits for sale. The scenery at the stations on the hills north of Bengal is grand. Simla and Missuri, 14,000 feet above the sea level. The air is pure and bracing, far above the mountains tower to 27,000 feet.

When the sun is setting in the west the view is splendid, as you see the glaciers reflecting a thousand different colours. Then to look down into the valleys below, far below, the roads are cut around the sides of the hills, and you journey up from hill to hill, like going round so many sugar loaves. Rose trees grow here to the size of oaks. The birds are of gorgeous plumage, such as the Argus pheasant, the Mango bird. The bantam fowl are numerous in the woods. Strawberries and nectarines are in abundance, growing on the sides of the hills. The natives bring in numbers of leopard and bear skins, also bears' grease. Butterflies are beautiful also; beetles of a large size, such as the elephant and stag beetle. I have made up cases of each that went at 16 *rupees* or 32 shillings. The mule is the only carrying animal who can travel round these roads with any safety. The ladies are conveyed in *jampans*, by four natives, a sort of palanquin, which swings on a pole.

All being arranged, the following day we marched to join Lord Gough, who with the main body are at Hureka Gaut. As we marched along the villagers generally welcomed us with *salaams*.

Lord Ellenborough had been succeeded as governor-general by Lord Hardinge. He, with General Gough, come out to meet Sir Harry and his division. We halted, and both rode along our front, giving us great praise for our victory at Aliwal on the 28th. We marched into camp, and occupied a position on the right of the army. Here we waited five days, worried with picket and guard duty, waiting for the siege guns being brought from Delhi by elephants. The enemy, we learned, were in a strong position, well fortified, a sort of half-moon, each horn resting on the Sutlej, with a bridge of boats in their rear, either to bring up supplies with, or to retreat by—under the command of Lall Sing, the Queen's favourite general. On the morning of the tenth of February we formed, an hour before daybreak, not a sound of trumpet or drum being heard. All was done silently.

At daybreak our mortars opened the ball by sending shell into the enemy's position. At six we were answered, and over two hundred pieces of ordnance roared away on both sides. A thirty-two pound ball, spent, struck one of our elephants, and as it was the first we saw wounded, we could not help laughing—indeed, the entire army burst into laughter—though to laugh in such a scene seems almost incredible. He had been hit on the rump, and to see him cantering and galloping over that field, upsetting everything almost he came across was indeed a sight.

On the same field a fox started between the two armies, and as the soldier's dog always follows him, one followed the fox, but from the confusion at the time I lost sight of them, though the fox stood some time confined, not knowing what way to get clear. At nine the infantry began their work by firing all along the line—the 31st ordered to charge at a break made by our guns, They did, and were repulsed by a heavy discharge of grape and canister. The 10th were then ordered to advance and take part, and in a short time both regiments, vieing with each other, made an entrance at the point of the bayonet, one of the 31st mounted on the breastwork with the British flag. It was completely perforated with shot, yet the man was charmed, for he was not touched. He afterwards got a commission.

The 16th Lancers with a battery of artillery, were ordered

up to command the bridge. The battery put in red-hot shot and destroyed the bridge. The centre boat forming the bridge was filled with combustibles. It was their intention, had they to retreat, to draw us away after them, and then blow us up. Now commenced hot work. We and the infantry got into their intrenched position. All fought like tigers, the Sikhs disputed every inch of ground down to the river bank, and into it while they could stand. They fought till about two o'clock, when the battle was ours. The river was all bloody and choked with bodies now added to those that had by this time floated down from Aliwal; and, strange, the water had risen two feet through the jamming caused by this obstruction. Thus ended the Battle of Sobraon, and with it the Sikh war of 1845-46.

Our loss was one hundred and fifty officers and eight hundred rank and file. General Dick was killed. The enemy left 16,000 dead and wounded on the field.

Our Engineers, on the 12th of February, constructed a bridge. We crossed over and marched towards their capital, Lahore. The country was in a deplorable state through the previous civil war. The agricultural and mercantile classes were ruined. As we neared the city, after a seven days' march, not knowing how we would be received, the principal chiefs and ministers made their appearance, bringing the young heir, Dulep, a boy, with them, and to make terms with the governor-general they were received in his Lordship's marquee, with a troop of the 9th and one of the 16th around inside the tent. They begged hard that the British flag should not float on the walls of Lahore, when his Lordship asked what compensation was to be had for the blood of his countrymen shed, when they, without provocation, invaded the Company's territory, "Yes," he added, without reply, "the flag of England shall float over your walls," he would crown the young *maharajah* and take the *doab*, the territory on the banks of the Sutlej up to Loodianna, as compensation for the expense such acts had entailed.

On the 21st we marched on to the plain in front of the city, and encamped opposite the gate called Delhi Gate. The city is surrounded by high walls flanked by towers mounting one hundred guns of large calibre, the whole surrounded by a deep moat. The River Ravie flows through the city. The most beautiful building was the Seraglio, the residence of the Rungeets, six hundred concubines. Many a fair woman was in there at that time, mostly from Circassia, captured by the Turcoman horse, in their raids among the Circassian villages, and brought to the fairs held in India every seven years for that purpose near the source of the Ganges.

On the 26th of February the young *maharajah* was crowned in the presence of the British Army and an immense throng of natives. The day following, Lall Sing came in with 10,000 of his troops and surrendered. They laid down their arms as they marched past us, our *sepoys* boasting they had defeated them. They retorted, saying, "No, you black pigs, but it was the Europeans who had. The English were brave, and they had fought them well." The Sikhs are a fine body of men—tall, good looking, and very proud. They had mostly been organized and drilled by French officers in Rungeit Sing's time, but after his death and the civil war commenced, the Frenchmen left, crossing to the Company's territories, some going home to France. It is certain Avitavula took his wife, who was the daughter of the Rungeit, and his daughter to Paris, to have them educated.

CHAPTER 7

Take Ship For South Africa

Peace was proclaimed on the 4th March, and Sir Henry Lawrence was appointed to remain as Resident, with a few of our troops, to protect the young king. On the following day Sir Harry Smith told us the commander-in-chief would now send us home, and volunteering would be opened for two regiments, the 3rd Light Dragoons and 9th Lancers. Any of us who chose might remain, however. Under the influence of *arrick*, a mad drink, the 9th got one, and the 3rd got ninety, of our men. The remnant, with the 31st Foot, left on the 8th of March for Calcutta. Before leaving, we were highly complimented by Lords Hardinge and Gough, and wished a safe voyage. Our bands struck up "Home, Sweet Home," and I remember how sweet the very sound of that air seemed so far away from home,—when one thought of the dear old land, and those dearer still who were uncertain as to whether most of us were living or dead.

Pushing on now, on a different errand, we recrossed the well-known Sutlej River, came to Ferosha, where we fought on the 22nd and 23rd December, 1845; and, after pitching tents, rambled over the field, one we had left in hot pursuit of the enemy. Words cannot be found to describe our horror on finding all around was still as death; not a living soul to be seen, the village completely deserted, heaps of men, horses and camels lying there for three months unburied; the infantry, just as they fell, clothed complete; the dragoons the same way accoutred and spurred; the horses and camels in the ditch just as they fell. We did as much as we could, and went on towards Meerut, where we arrived on the 2nd May, being met by the band of the 14th Light Dragoons, who played us to the station. We were seven weeks from Lahore.

Giving up our horses, we made all preparations for home by Calcutta, 900 miles from Meerut. We now sold our library, distributing the proceeds, together with the benevolent and canteen fund, among the men. This, with our prize money, after being separately awarded, was sent to our army agents in London, to be drawn when we reached home. On the 8th of May we started on foot for Gurmatesa Gaut, on the Ganges, just three days' march, where we were to take boats for Calcutta. Before embarking on the Ganges, a despatch was received from Lord Gough appointing our Colonel, Cureton, adjutant-general of the army in Bengal. He bade us a sorrowful goodbye, saying he came out with the regiment in 1822, hoped to go home with them, but this promotion frustrated that. "All the honours I have," said he, "and all the promotions I have received, I attribute to the brave men of the 16th."

All shook hands with him, some went so far as to embrace him, and tears were shed, for he was a father to his men. We had a strange voyage down the Ganges, the water being low at this time of the year, and our men did almost as they pleased, so joyful were they at the prospect of going home. Few officers accompanied us, as many went over land to England. Sailing at night was dangerous, our boats were therefore moored; sandbars, stumps of immense trees, and an accumulation of rubbish met us everywhere. Our time was generally passed shooting flying-foxes, monkeys, alligators.

We as often shot dead bodies as living, the Hindoos consigning all the dead to the waters of their goddess, Ganga. We reached Dum Dum, twelve miles from Calcutta, on 29th July, 1846, and as the ship at Calcutta was not ready, while she was getting so we took up quarters in the artillery barracks at this station. Here we had a grand ball given by the citizens, and at which our newly-appointed colonel and a sergeant's wife made the only couple who came out with the regiment. We had all the grandees of Calcutta up at it. Every tree for miles was illuminated; dancing was kept up all night. At this ball I met a young friend, who had been a comrade of mine, when he was one of us, but who, fortunately, had got married to a wealthy heiress, and was now settled near Calcutta, in a most beautiful mansion. I have introduced the reader before to Calcutta, but it was only a bird's-eye view from on board ship; now, however, as I had leisure to visit it and walk through its streets, I may give a more detailed description of it. Most of the wealthy people live outside, in the suburbs, such as the Dum Dum or Barrackpoor road.

The city itself covers an area of sixteen square miles, and has some fine streets; the principal ones, at each corner have stands, where you can hire a *pallankeen* for a *rupee*, or two shillings, a day, to go shopping or visiting; four waiters carry it, two in front and two behind. They are beautifully got up, lined with silk cushions and generally have a crimson blind. The old city is of bamboo structure, thatched roofs, mostly inhabited by the lower order of natives. In the city proper the buildings are large and hand-some, built mostly of brick, some of stone and marble. The brick houses seem very old, as if they had been built at a very early pe-riod. It is quite common to see elephants, mostly bearing some wealthy *rajah* in his *howda*, gorgeously attired, towards the water front. They are quite commonly used drawing heavy burdens, logs, &c. It is hardly credible, but they are so sagacious as to be used in bringing messages. I mean such as going alone for water. Camels may be met in strings bringing goods from all points of India. In the evening, the mall of Calcutta is the common cool resort. Here you may see all the fashionables, and people from all parts of the earth. The bazaars are very numerous; in any of them you can purchase for a small sum any article you require. There are also some very fine hotels

On the 14th of August we marched to Calcutta to embark, two hundred and eighty-seven men all told. This was the rem-nant of eight hundred who marched to the Panjaub in 1845. The hottest day ever known in India was the day we embarked. Twelve men fell dead from the excess of heat; indeed, the au-thorities were blamed for ordering us out on such a day, on account of having some men who had been wounded, and a number of women and children on board. The captain put to sea at once, to avoid, if possible, any further sickness.

On the 19th we got clear into the Bay of Bengal. The monsoons set in, and we had a succession of storms for three weeks. We cleared in good time Point de Galle; rounded Cape of Good Hope in the beginning of October, and ran for St. Helena. Here we took in fresh water. A French man-of-war, with troops from the island of Bourbon, anchored alongside of us. Of course, we fraternized as well as we possibly could, but the associations connected with St. Helena and England were not then as well smoothed down as now. The island stands alone like a large lock in mid-ocean. Passing the island of Ascension, nothing particular occurred till our arrival in the British Channel, on 23rd December, 1846. By daylight we looked on the land we loved, and saw patches of snow here and there, and as we had seen none for fifteen years, it was a sight we enjoyed.

We felt all warmed up, and hearts beat high when we saw the white cliffs of Dover. We waited off Deal for a pilot, and being surrounded by bumboats, we found a difference in the desire to cheat with exorbitant prices for bread, butter or cheese, to what we had been used to by native Indians. The Ramsgate tug came off and took us to Gravesend, where we arrived on the evening of the 28th. Hundreds of boats put off, filled with relatives—mothers, sisters, brothers and old sweethearts—to welcome the living heroes, or hear some sad talk of the absent. The sight was heartrending in some instances. One poor mother, hearing of her son having been killed at Sobraon, threw herself into the water, frantic, and with difficulty was rescued. In the afternoon two war steamers took us aboard for Herne Bay, to save us the march, as our station was Canterbury, and it was distant from the bay only seven miles.

On landing, one of the men fell out, and actually knelt and kissed the ground, a bystander in the crowd saying, "Bless his soul, how he loves the old sod;" and many came and shook hands, not only with him but with all within reach. Omnibuses and waggons were ready for the sick, and women and children. We got leave to breakfast for a short time, and what a rush for the hotels. Storming an enemy's fort was nothing to it. Assembling at nine, we marched to Canterbury. Here, the Mayor and Corporation, accompanied by two bands, came to meet us. Between laurel branches in profusion, music from two bands, crowds of ladies and gentlemen in carriages, citizens on foot shouting, huzzahing and handkerchief-waving, we got a right royal reception in the famous old city; and as the officers commanding considered it no use to close the gates, or attempt to confine us within walls, we were allowed two days' leave, to do as we pleased.

On the first of January I received my month's furlough. I started for London. The day was very cold and snowing; how pleasant for me, just home from the hottest spot on earth. A cab soon brought me to Westminster, where my parents resided; I reached home at half-past eleven a.m. My sisters, when I left, were children, in those few years had grown women. One of them opened the door in answer to my knock, and fainted on seeing one of the 16th, not perhaps that she recognized me, as I was bronzed with the sun and heavily bearded. This brought my mother; dear old mother, how one does get fond of mother, when separated from her, and away, as I was in India, from her kind care. Ah, mother, I remember you yet, though I am old now, as you fell into my arms, and almost swooned. My sisters had to remove her, till by the aid of restoratives they got her round; then, such a look, sadness and joy combined. It was me, though the many reports of the fearful suffering of my regiment, she could believe until she saw me herself, whether her eyes would ever see her son again. Yes, mother.

Thy image is still—the dearest impressed on my heart,
And the tablet so faithful—in death must be still
Ere a trace of that image departs.

My father was, of course, rejoiced to see me, and so were all my old friends and acquaintances. The charges of Aliwal and Sobraon were in every one's mouth, and as I was the only man on leave near my home, I had many an enquiry how I felt, and how this and that was done.

In this way, a month, the extent of my furlough, was not long

66

THE ASCENT TO THE TEMPLE OF PARBUTTEE, NEAR POONA
(FROM ORIGINAL EDITION)

in passing, and I had to rejoin my regiment. I might have stated before, I was in full charge of my troop all the way home; we had no officers, and I was the senior sergeant. The reader will therefore be as much surprised as I was, on joining my corps, to find the vacancy of troop serjeant-major filled by the promotion of a man from the depôt, without any fault whatever to me, as I was fully competent in every respect, but merely to please the whim of some depôt officer. I was very much stung to think I was the only serjeant left alive at Aliwal, had brought my men home, and that one who had never crossed the English Channel should be promoted over me.

From Canterbury we went to Deal, as a riot was feared at the election. Here we met our old comrades, the 31st Foot, just home from India. In May, 1847, we were ordered to Brighton, in Sussex. Our route lay through Battle, near Hastings, where William the Conqueror defeated Harold, paying a visit to the Abbey. Here the King (Harold) was buried; his tomb is over-grown with ivy. An ancient painting of the battle may be seen in the great hall, with two statues of Saxon warriors on each side. We reached Brighton on the seventh of May. In this fashionable watering-place we commemorated the second anniversary of Aliwal with a grand ball, at which were the Duke of Wellington, Prince Albert, the officers of all the Guards regiments, and the fashionables from the Metropolis; the pavilion was filled on the occasion—twenty of our troopers, medal-men, lining the grand stairway. One entire regiment went to the theatre, where Jenny Lind sang.

Fearing a Chartist riot in London, at a great meeting to be held on Kensington Common, we were ordered up on the 10th April. We stopped two days, and then proceeded, three troops to Ipswich, five to Norwich. Here we remained till the spring of 1849, breaking young horses, and getting ready for a grand review by Her Majesty. In May we got the route for Hounslow, one troop to Kensington, to do Royal Escort duty. I had the honour of being one of the escort of Her Majesty on the 24th May, from Nine-Elms station to Buckingham Palace. On the 26th following, before the Iron Duke, Prince Albert, Her Majesty, and a host of the aristocracy, we paraded and went through a field-day, charging as we did at Aliwal, and only stopped with the horses' heads over the carriage of Her Majesty. Here, after the review, she pinned on our breasts the Medals for the Punjaub.

Not feeling exactly pleased as to the way I was treated, after many days' serious consideration, I determined to leave the regiment, as I could now claim a free discharge, having completed twelve years' service. I might have remained till my time of double service had expired, when I would be entitled to a pension. Stung by seeing a man my serjeant-major who should not be, and knowing I had earned the step well, I applied for my discharge at once. The colonel met me with apologies and excuses, promising to recommend me for a commission, and so on, but feeling the position, if I did get it, would be more than I could manage, on the pay which I would have to support my rank on, I declined, and in time got what I asked for, leaving the corps almost heart-broken.

In July following I got the appointment of steward, East India United Service Club, in London, and entered upon those duties immediately. In June, 1850, a gentleman whom I saw at the Club was going to settle in South Africa. He intended to breed horses, and had selected a large tract of land at Georgetown, on the Nysena River, for that purpose. With him I made an engagement, sailing on the good ship *Devonshire,* on the 15th July, and as I was fortunate in India to arrive on the breaking out of hostilities, so the reader will find I was equally fortunate on reaching the Cape, though a civilian, to find men were wanted to stem the insurrection and rebellious spirit of the Kaffirs, which is portrayed in the next chapter.

CHAPTER 8

The Religion of the Hindoos

Before proceeding further in this work, it will be interesting to the reader to understand something of the religion, what it springs from, and the certain peculiarities in the intermixture of the several Hindoo families, giving rise to the several castes and ranks to which each is born to, and in which they must continue, or progress by marriage in the higher scale when allowed by their code of laws. I have been to a great deal of trouble in procuring this information, as it is not found in many writings of that country, and will, therefore, be new to a great many.

From the earliest period of which any records are extant, the Hindoo races have been divided as a people into four distinct classes or castes, designated Brahmins, Kshatriyas, Vaisyas and Sudras, originating with the creation of the world. Brahmins, according to their mythological creed, proceeding from the mouth of Brahma, the creator, the chief person of their theological belief—his mission was to rule and instruct. He formed the caste distinguished by the name Kshatriyas, which means sprung from the arms—of Brahma: and this deity's duty was to protect. Vaisyas, from his thighs; and the province allotted to this emanation of the deity was to trade, and cultivate the earth. Sudra, the most abject, as produced from the feet of Brahma, was doomed to be the servant or slave of the superior caste; the four forming the yet existing classes or castes of priests—soldiers, husbandmen or traders, and labourers.

The division of these four classes are, however, extended; and in the fourteenth century b.c. the number of mixed classes recognized by their laws of Menu had become very considerable, Of these we may mention the classes which have sprung from the marriage of a man of the upper caste with a woman of an inferior class.

1st, Murdhabhishicta, by a Brahmin with a woman of the Kshatriya class: his duty is to teach military exercises.

2nd, Ambastha, by a Brahmin from a woman of the Vaisya class or caste: he is a medicine man.

3rd, Nishadhu, by a Brahmin from a woman of the Sudra class: his occupation is to catch fish.

4th, Mahishya, by a Kshatriya from a woman of the Vaisya class: his profession is music, astronomy and attendance on cattle.

5th, Ugra, by a Kshatriya from a woman of the Sudra class: his duty, according to Menu, is to kill or confine such animals as live in holes: he is also a bard or poet.

6th, Carana, by a Vaisya from a woman of the Sudra class: he is an attendant on princes, or secretary.

The classes which have sprung from a marriage of a woman of the upper caste with a man of inferior caste is again subdivided, and the offspring of such is considered inferior than the other, and also illegitimate.

1st, we will say Sota, by a Kshatriya from a woman of Brahmin rank: his occupation is managing horses and driving carts.

2nd, Vaidscha, by a Vaisya from a woman of the Brahmin class: his occupation is a waiter on women.

3rd, Chandola, by a Sudra from a woman of the Brahmin class: he is regarded the most impure of the whole race, and his business is to handle dead bodies, execute animals, and to officiate in the most abject employment.

4th, Mahada, by a Vaisya from a Kshatriya woman: his profession is, according to Menu, travelling with merchandise; he is also an economist or bard.

5th, Asygara, by a Sudra from a woman of the Vaisya class; he is a carpenter. And there is another class, Kohatti, by a Sudra from a Kshadriya woman: his occupation is killing or confining animals who live in trees.

There are also other classes descending in the scale of impurity from mixed marriages. One of those most known is that of Pariahs; they are subject to labour of agriculture and to the filthiest duty of scavengers. With these there is no intercourse allowed, nor can one show the least sympathy for them, no matter how low or depressed they may be;

The faith of these several castes centres in a triune godhead, Brahma the centre, Vishnu the preserver or sustainer, and Siva the destroyer. Brahma, the superior, always remains in holy solitude in the distance of the caste profound of measureless space, and is beyond the reach of superstition to profane by even ideal similitude; Vishnu and Siva are supposed to have been many times incarnate, and hence the imagination of the Hindoo has clothed them with a variety of visible forms, and each has become a distinct deity, to whom worship is daily addressed. The Hindoo Pantheon also includes a host of inferior deities or divinities.

Nothing can be done without supernatural intervention, in consequence of which the elements, and every variety of animated nature, are placed under the immediate guardianship of one of the crowd of deities that throng the Brahmanical heaven. The goodly company is further augmented by myriads of demi-gods, many of whom are of the most wretched description. Thus, a little red paint smeared over a block of wood, a shapeless stone, or a lump of clay, makes it a deity, and a number of such monstrosities collected together indicate a Brahmin place of worship, and invite to some act of worship as debasing in its nature as its object is monstrous in conception.

Among the animals which are the objects of Hindoo worship or adoration, and one that I shall have to refer to often, is the cow. This is the most sacred in most parts of India. The cow is frequently termed the "Mother of the gods," and many are kept by the well-to-do Hindoo for the sole purpose of worship. Circumstances are, however, at times even stronger than superstition itself, and then the poor, who derive their chief support from the labour of this useful animal so venerated, do not hesitate to work it hard and to feed it very sparingly.

Besides the peculiar notions entertained by the Hindoo relative to superior beings and the worship to be paid them, those that refer to a future state form a prominent part of their theological system. Here the doctrine of transmigration of souls is a distinguishing feature. No people appear to have formed loftier ideas of its nature independently of its connection with matter. They carry the idea to so extravagant a height as to suppose the souls of both men and brute animals to have been originally portions of the Supreme mind, and consequently as participating in its eternity. The highest destiny to which a mortal can aspire is therefore reabsorbed into the divine essence, where the Hindoo's idea of supreme felicity receives its perfection, and the mind reposes on an unruffled sea of bliss.

But to such a state only the most rigid ascetics who have spent a life of self-inflicted torture can aspire, the best deeds of an ordinary life cannot excite a hope of raising their author higher than one of the various heavens over which their multiplied divinities separately preside. But few are allowed to cherish the expectation of ascending to even the lowest of these, and the great body of believers have only to anticipate the consolations that flow from the transmigration of souls.

As regards punishment, a series have been devised to suit the capabilities of the people and the irregular propensities of life. The institutes of Menu affirm that he who steals grain in the husk becomes a rat—should he take water, he is to be a diver—if honey, a large gnat, and if flesh, he is transformed into a vulture. The next bath of one who steals a deer or elephant is into a wolf, and if a carriage, the thief is sure to become a camel. When once sunk from the human to the brute creation, the Parana's assert that he must pass through many millions of baths before he regains the human form. Their system of punishment is not however confined to these terrestrial transgressions. The all-multiplying system of the Hindoo theology has created a hundred thousand hells for those whom inferior evils could not deter from the commission of more heinous crimes.

When the fatal moment arrives which changes their present

position, they are hurried away through the space of 688,000 miles among the faithful rocks and eternal snows of the Himalaya mountains to the judgement seat of Yoma, where the god messengers await to convey them to their respective places of punishment, and here, too, the state of retribution is adapted to the nature of the crime. The murderer is fed on flesh and blood; the adulterer is to be embraced by an image of red-hot iron, and the unmerciful to be unceasingly bitten by snakes. Having endured this state of "penal servitude" for a period proportionate to the magnitude of their crimes, the first step to restoration is to pass a long series of ages in the form of some degraded animal, whence they ascend to the scale of being already described.

CHAPTER 9

Delhi the Ancient Capital
of the Mogul Empire

Delhi being the ancient capital of the Mogul Empire, I will here give a description of it, as, having a few days leave from cantonment, I found it in my visit. It is situated on the eastern bank of the Jumna, and some 950 miles from Calcutta. It is walled and fortified, and has a population of somewhere near 200,000. It is between seven and eight miles round it, and may be about two miles across. The palace inhabited by the king stands in a very commanding position. The entire city is built on a rocky range of hills, and, as said, is surrounded by embattled walls and guns, with intervening Martello towers facing along the whole extent with good masonry, moats and glacis. Its chief houses are built of brick, the streets narrow; the principal avenues all wide and handsome, and for an Asiatic city, very clean. The bazaars along the avenues look remarkably pretty; formerly the city had some noble wide streets, but these have been divided by buildings all along the centre, and now spoil their appearance.

The next principal buildings to the palace is the Jumna Musjeed, or chief mosque. The tombs of the Emperor Humayoon, and of Sefjar Jung, and Cuttub Menir; and within the new city are the remains of many palaces. These structures are nearly all of red granite inlaid and ornamented with white marble; the general style is elegant, yet simple. The palace, as seen from a distance, is very high, with gothic towers and battlements rising above any other building. It was built by Shah Jehan, and seems some sixty feet high, with two noble gateways. It is allowed by travellers to far surpass the *Kremlin*, in Moscow, in magnificence, or any other kingly residence. I thought, on looking at it, of our old Windsor Castle, and asked did any of them making the comparison ever see it. To my mind old Windsor surpasses it, except in its material.

The gardens known as the Shelima, and mentioned in Lalla Rookh, were formed by the same potentate, and are said to have cost the immense sum of 1,000,000 pounds; but they are now wild and allowed to go in ruins. The Mosque-Musjeed is considered the largest and most elegant temple of worship in India, it cost sixty lacks of *rupees*, and Shah Jehan was six years in building it. It stands on a rocky eminence scarped for the purpose. A flight of thirty-five steps brings you to a beautiful gateway of red stones, the doors of which are covered with wrought brass.

The terrace on which it is built is about 1600 yards square, and surrounded by an arched colonnade with pavilions at convenient distances. In the centre stands a large marble cistern supplied by machinery with water from the canal. On the west side of the Mosque proper, of an oblong form, say 260 feet in length, its entire front is coated with large slabs of white marble, and compartments in the comer are inlaid with Arabic inscriptions in black. The mosque is approached by another flight, and surrounded by a marble dome at the flanks, as at all mosques, are minarets about 150 feet high, each having three projecting galleries of black marble and red stone alternately, their summits crowned with light pavilions of white marble. The ascent is by winding stairs of 180 steps of red stone. It is truly a noble structure, well worth this unequal description—for it must be seen to realize its beauty. It is said this mosque is maintained by a grant from our Government.

Not far from the king's palace is another of red stone, used I suppose by that personage and his princes for intermediate times of worship. This one is surmounted with three gilt domes. Altogether there is some fifty mosques in this city, of more or less grandeur, some bear marks of great antiquity. One other, however, deserves a note in passing, and that one was erected in

1710 by the daughter of the great and mighty Arungzebee, and in which she is buried. Perhaps the oldest is the one erected by the ancient Patans or Afghan conquerors of India. It is of dark coloured granite, and of a different design, but exactly like the Arab mosques.

The prospect south of the Shulnia gardens, as far as the eye can reach, is covered with the remains of extensive gardens, pavilions, sepulchres, all connecting the town of Cattab with the capital, and through their neglected appearance, exhibiting one of the most striking scenes of desolation to be witnessed.

The celebrated Cattab Minar is a very handsome round tower rising from a polygon of twenty-seven sides, in five different stages, gradually diminishing in circumference to the height of 250 feet, its summit crowned with a majestic cupola rising from four arcades of red granite is reached by a spiral staircase of 384 steps, and between each stage a balcony runs round the pillar. The Patan, erected by the old conquerors is almost in ruins, it was once a solid fortress, its architecture not sinking, but there remains a high black pillar of metal of Hindoo construction, originally covered with inscriptions.

I have before alluded to the tomb of Humayoon the conqueror, which was erected by his daughter. It is of gothic architecture, and stands in an immense garden with terraces and numerous fountains; everything about it bears marks of decay. The garden is surrounded by an embattled wall and cloister, and in its centre, on a platform ascended by a flight of granite steps, is the tomb itself, a square building with circular apartments, surrounded by a dome of white marble. From the top of this building the ruins all round can best be seen—where Indrapat once stood—extending almost over a range of hills seven or eight miles distant.

The soil in the neighbourhood of Delhi seems singularly devoid of vegetation. The Jumna annually overflows its banks during the rainy season, but its waters, in this part of its course, are so much empregnated with natron that the ground is almost barren. In order to supply water to the royal gardens, the aqueduct of Ali-Khan was constructed through the chief avenue, by which the pure and wholesome water was brought from the mountains, over one hundred and twenty miles off. This channel, during the troubles that followed the decline of the Mogul Empire was stopped by rubbish, but when the English got possession they cleared it, and it is now the sole source of supply of Delhi. This was done in 1820, and is still remembered by the inhabitants with, I trust, some degree of gratitude. It was, at least, on the opening of the channel, for the inhabitants then turned out, with drums beating, to welcome the water, throwing flowers, and *ghee*, and sweetmeats in the current as it flowed along; for this they called down all manner of blessings on the British. But for this dearth of water, Delhi would be a great inland mart for the interchange of commodities between India and the countries west and north.

Cotton, cloth and indigo are manufactured here, and there is also a large Persian shawl factory, with weavers from Cashmere. The bazaars rival any others in wealth and beauty. At the south of the city stand the ruins of an observatory, erected by Jye Singh; it formerly contained several instruments, but, like the building, long ago partially destroyed. There is also a college in this city, with two departments—Orientals and English—and the number of pupils are 270. I have dwelt rather long on this description of the famous city, but I feel any picture I can give will be far short of the reality.

It is said seven cities, at different times of the earth's history, have stood on the same site. Indrapat was the first; then the Patans, or Afghans; then Sultan Balun built and fortified one, after destroying the Patans; then Mozes-ud-deem built another nearer the Jumna; this destroyed, another nearer Cattal; and lastly. Shah Jehan, towards the middle of the seventeenth century, chose the present site for his capital.

I might add that the census of any place in India is hardly ever taken, for the reason of so much superstition in the inhabitants—they could not be made to believe anything else but that it was intended for their destruction. The estimate of the population I have given was then considered as nearly as possible correct.

Calcutta presents a remarkable instance of what may arise from small beginnings, if I might so speak. In 1640 the English obtained permission to erect a factory at the ancient town of Hooghly, on the opposite bank of the river. In 1696 the Emperor Aurungzcebee allowed them to remove to the pretty village of Govindpoor, and in the following year to secure it by erecting a fort. So slow was the progress of the new settlement that up to 1717 the site of the present City of Palaces remained an assemblage of huts, wretched indeed, with only a few hundred inhabitants. In 1756 it had not more than seventy houses in it occupied by the English. An attempt had been made in 1742 to defend the place from the invasion of the Maharattas, by surrounding it with a ditch, a precaution, however, which availed but little against the attack, in June, 1756, by Suradja-ud-douhal, or Viceroy of Bengal. In consequence of this attack, apparently a surprise, the factory was deserted by the governor, the commandant and many of the European functionaries and residents.

A memorable catastrophe of a most lamentable nature ensued. Such of the English as had remained for its defence were seized and thrust into a small uninhabited dungeon called the Black-hole, and of one hundred and forty-six individuals who were thus shut up at night, one hundred and twenty three perished under the most frightful sufferings ere the arrival of morning. The Black-hole was afterwards converted into a warehouse, and upon an obelisk, fifty feet high at its entrance, were inscribed the names of the unhappy victims.

Early in the following year a squadron of five ships brought 2,400 troops under Lord Clive up the Hooghly from Madras, they retook the town of Calcutta, from which the garrison of the Subidhar retired after an attack of only two hours duration. The population now amounts to some 600,000.

CHAPTER 10

War Rumours

Favoured with beautiful weather, and nothing having occurred to mar our passage, we sighted the Cape on the twentieth of October. As the high land comes first to view, it has all the appearance of a lion *couchant*—the flag-staff rising from the lion's tail, creeping round the point to a narrow entrance, the whale rock and Robin Island come in view, then Cape Town stretches before you, in a sort of basin. Table Mountain at the back, the town sloping up from the bay, with the Blue Berg Mountains away to the east. At this time of year summer commences in the Cape. We had, therefore, a summer Christmas before us. Landing on the twenty-sixth, we took up quarters in the Pier hotel. Steamers did not venture on such long voyages in those days, and the influx of visitors was not so great as now. Living we found very cheap; a bottle of wine, and very good at that, cost four-pence; British brandy, sixpence, it was called "Cape-smoke;" meat was two-pence per pound; peaches, pomegranates and grapes, one shilling per basket—bushel.

The villa residences on the outskirts are very pretty—the fences surrounding them are either rose or geranium bushes, standing as high as six feet; or cactus, or prickly pear. The inhabitants of the Colony are mostly of Dutch descent, or Malays. Originally it was a slave settlement. Hither they were brought from Batavia—but on the British Government assuming control, slavery was abolished. The descendants of these are now the most industrious, as they are the wealthiest inhabitants. Their principal occupation is, or was then, whaling and seal-fishing, with some tradesmen among them. The aborigines of the Cape, or Hottentots, are a low, degraded, idle class.

Our old East Indian friend and General, Sir Harry Smith, I found here as governor-general and commander-in-chief of the Colony of South Africa—and it was here, and at such a time, too, such an experienced soldier was required. Sandilla, a Gaika chief, had commenced hostilities on the frontier, and his *kaffirs* had burnt over twenty farms, butchered the farmers and their families, and carried off all their cattle. Though now free from the service, it was but natural, after my previous service, I should feel interested in anything concerning military movements or threatenings of war, and I soon made myself acquainted with all the particulars. The entire British force in the Colony consisted of three infantry battalions. These were scattered in detachments all over the country, only the headquarters of the 73rd were at Cape Town.

The Governor and his staff, taking these, left for the scene of disturbance, and levies were ordered all over. Besides the atrocities mentioned, the *kaffirs* had murdered all the men in the three military villages of Auckland, Wobown and Joanisburgh. I could not be expected to remain long unknown, as, having seen service in the Sixteenth Lancers in India, was surprised by a request from the Colonial Secretary to assist in raising levies, who offered me a command as lieutenant in the Second Corps of Europeans. A draft of two hundred men, with seventy-eight horses, was ordered up to East London, and having given my consent, I was sent in charge.

On the first of February I went on board the war steamer *Hermes*, with that number, and left for the frontier. On reaching East London, we found we could get no nearer than about two miles. Anchoring, surf-boats were brought alongside, and in these, after immense trouble, all were safely landed. Well, I had seen many towns and forts, and I have been in towns since called after our beautiful capital, but such a place as this aspiring to the great name, surprised me. The whole place consisted of one building, called a hotel; four huts; four commissariat houses; and a small fort, with a dozen or so *kaffirs*, apparently friendly, standing round-about naked, fine, manly-looking fellows, copper coloured, and all six feet high or thereabouts. We found the army was encamped at Fort William, eighteen miles from East London. I marched in charge of my detachment of men and horses, to which was added a convoy of thirty-six waggons loaded with provisions.

We halted at Fort Murry, half-way. Captain McLean, of the 6th Foot, was in charge here with one company. We were now in a friendly chief's country; his name was Patto. Having been detained longer than was expected by the slow travel of the bullock waggons, it was late next afternoon when we reached the camp at King William Fort. The next day being Sunday, I was ordered to parade my men before General Sir Harry Smith—after which, and being quite satisfied with his inspection, and some conversation about old times, he ordered my rank to be confirmed as lieutenant, 2nd Corps Cape Town Levies.

Having had some time to rest, I was enabled to scan about me, and see a little of the place and people. Here I had an opportunity of seeing that dreadful bush so much spoken of—*Kaffir* land—and it is a bush—so dense, and thick, and so full of the Momossa tree, with its long thorns, it is almost impossible to penetrate. As one moved any distance round, plenty of women and girls might be seen; they come up the valleys with immense pumpkins, corn, or milk, to exchange for beads, buttons, or, in fact, anything strange. As they don't know the use of money, an old brass ring would buy all one wanted for a day.

They were quite as oblivious of dress as the men we had first seen, only a small apron of deerskin around their waste. Some had blankets. They looked horrible, so full of red clay for paint, and they were disgustingly dirty. The Hottentots or Aborigines' worth is all in cattle. The women feed them, build their own houses, sow the corn, and do all the drudgery. The men do nothing but hunt, and in war time fight. The boys are not allowed to associate with men until after circumcision, which takes place at eighteen; then they may sit round the council fire with the men.

I found our army composed of volunteers from Cape Town

district, Mossel Bay and Grahamstown—in all some 20,000 Europeans, Hottentots and Fingoes, besides the British 6th and 73rd Regiments. The Cape mounted riflemen had, a few days previous to our arrival, most of them at least, gone over to the enemy, taking their horses and arms. They had intended to massacre all the 73rd Regiment the night previous, while they were asleep; this was frustrated through a friendly chief giving information to Sir Harry Smith, and it was thought strange that all the Hottentots of Wesleyan mission stations remained loyal, when those situated east, under missionaries of other denominations, joined the insurgents; these proved our worst foes, being such good marksmen.

All arrangements being completed, we broke camp and marched towards the River Kiskama, then crossed into the Gaika territory to hunt up Sandilla. Here we remained three weeks, engaged in skirmishing and picket duty, the *kaffirs* troubling us much at night, firing from the bush. This kind of warfare is most disliked by the soldier—every bush containing an enemy, and no sooner you made one than they were off to another. In fact, they were always near us, particularly at night, and yet we could get no chance of having a good shot at them. The *kraal*, better known now than ever before, is a collection of huts, made in the form of large beehives, placed in a circle—the cattle in the middle—we invariably burned them. They were erected in some sheltered place, on the sides of hills or mountains.

We were now on the territory of the most powerful chief, Sandilla, head of the Gaikas. Reinforcements joined us here from England—the 43rd Foot, 60th Rifles and 12th Lancers; and General Sir Harry Smith, considering he had troops sufficient, ordered an advance on Fuller's-hook, and the Water-kloof where he had learned Sandilla had massed some thirty-thousand warriors. General Somerset was at this time at Fort Beaufort. At Fuller's-hook we had some terrible bush fighting, but succeeded in driving them into Water-kloof. The intricacies of this place, and the dense bush, it is almost impossible to describe. Here we remained some six weeks, and were joined by the 74th from Grahamstown, under Colonel Fordyce, who was shot on the top of the *kloof.*

Our advancement during that time in the progress, of the war was very little, as we could get no open field-fight, they proving as able as their opponents in bushwhacking. Sir Harry, seeing little progress marched us back to King Williamstown. Here the general sent for me, and ordered a start at twelve that night with 100 men—*Fingoes*—and fifty of Armstrong's horse, to capture 800 head of cattle in the Buffalo. Port Sandilla was said to be with them. With my command, I made a rapid march so as to reach before daybreak the place appointed, and arrived at the foot of the mountain half-an-hour before sunrise. The Buffalo Port I found a deep basin in the hills, the ascent very difficult and dense with bush. This basin had an outlet called the Gether Goolie, or Wolfs throat. With my men, I ascended the hill as best I could, leaving some mounted men at the Pass to hold the cattle.

On the word "charge," down the hill we went, amid a volley from the *kaffirs*, who were almost indistinguishable. I received a cut from an assaigai, knocking me off my horse, stunning me for a time. Soon, however, I recovered sufficient to stay the wound—remounted and joined my men, who by this time had joined the men below at the Pass. Here, too, the Fingoes had the cattle. Handing them over to the mounted men, we hurried on to the Yellow-wood—pursued by the *kaffirs*. On the following morning we reached King Williamstown, having lost two men killed and nine wounded. During that day's engagement we were hard pressed. It, however, nearly cost the *kaffirs* their leader, Sandilla—as one of our men had shot his horse, and nearly captured himself. There was a £1,000 on his head.

In July I was ordered, with fifty Europeans and Lieutenant Fielding with one hundred Hottentots Levy, to the Bridle Neck bush, on the road to East London, to protect convoys of prisoners coming by sea. The enemy, knowing this, lay in ambush to attack the waggons, and on returning we had to build stockades by cutting huge trees and sinking them four feet in the ground, leaving them four feet out, with the waggons inside for the night. This was trying work, and watching all night against a surprise. However, the duty was well done, and the convoy escorted safe through the dense bush.

The time of the men who had joined for six months having more than expired, I was ordered to take some five hundred of them to Cape Town, on the war steamer *Styx*. I had orders to raise and bring back as many mounted men as I could get, at a bounty of twenty-three pounds and free rations, finding their own horses, and rations were to be given them. It was chiefly expected my contingent would consist of farmers' sons, and such like, who, for their own interests, would join the army formed for the protection of their own homes. After seeing the discharged men paid, I started on my recruiting errand, and soon got together sixty men from Wooster, Swellingdam and Clanwilliam, mostly sons of Europeans.

The Affricandas, as they are called, are good riders and fine shots. When at Clanwilliam, I stayed with Mr. Shaw, and while out with him one day, we came across the greatest herd of deer I ever saw. We came on the opening of an immense plain, and for miles one could see swarms of gnu, elands, heart-beasts, rye-buck, bonti-buck, blue-buck, and other common deer. It was explained to me when there is a drought and scarcity of provisions in the Karoo they are driven down to seek water and the Salt licks. They are as bad as locusts to the farmer, not leaving a blade of grass where they visit; consequently, they turn out and destroy them as best they can, take their skins off, remove the best of the beef to dry it for home use, leaving the carcase for the wild dogs and lions.

The farmers in South Africa generally hold from ten to twenty thousand acres of land, with large flocks of sheep, and numbers of brood-mares; in the eastern part, and in the western, they mostly cultivate the grape for wine. There being no hotels in the country parts, and the farmhouses consequent on their large holdings, very far apart, during the long rides the screeching of the guinea fowl, together with the cooing of the turtle-dove, constantly salute the ear. When you stop under the shade of some trees to make coffee, it is easy to have a dainty bit of some wild bird to satisfy hunger, by going a few yards and killing one. In my travels going east, I have met dozens of waggons at a time going to Cape Town with wool, hides, horns, bitter aloes, and gums. The Hottentots employed as shepherds by these farmers seem fit for nothing else, an idle, lazy, indolent race. Some are squatted on every farm for that purpose, acting as shepherds.

On my journey I came across packs of wild dogs. These animals prove a great enemy to the farmer—worrying his sheep. It may not seem truth, but there are in this part of the country people of very small stature, wild, almost savage, at least bordering on the brute called Bosjesmen, living in holes in the rocks, who are adepts with bow and arrow, the latter of which they poison when at war. They live chiefly on the wild dog; snakes do not come even amiss to them. Europeans class them between the ape and the man. Darwin may have founded his theory on them—evolution. We will leave it with him, as beyond our solution.

As soon as I procured all the recruits I could, I started for Cape Town, and embarked on board the war steamer *Styx*, Captain Hall, for East London. On arriving we were soon joined by one hundred horses and men from Port Elizabeth, and again left for headquarters with one hundred and twenty waggons of stores and ammunition. While *en route* we learned of the loss of the steamer *Birkenhead*, as she was coming out of Simon's Bay with troops, drafts mostly for our army. Very few escaped that fearful wreck. Arriving at the headquarters of the army, the corps was named the "Montague Horse," in compliment to the Colonial Secretary, Sir John Montague. Many of these men were independent farmers.

CHAPTER 11

Transferred to Fingoe Service

In February, 1852, I was transferred to the Fort Peddie Fingoe Levy, under Captain J. Fainton. The Fingoes are a tribe formerly conquered and kept in bondage by the Amagahekas, but released by the British, and located at the fort of that name, near Grahamstown. They are very loyal, industrious, and make fine farm servants to the Scotch settlers on the frontier. So trustworthy are they, many are employed as police. Understanding the traits of the *kaffir* character, they are very useful, particularly as they hold a grudge against their old oppressors. Sir Harry Smith, having learned the enemy had sent all their cattle across the Kye River to Chief Krielle, Colonel Eyre, of the 73rd, was ordered, in conjunction with a squadron the 12th Lancers, under Major Tottenham, two troops Montague Horse, with all the infantry, consisting of 73rd, 43rd, and 60th Rifles, and my company of Fingoes, to capture them, punishing the Chief Krielle for his deception, as he had given his adhesion to the British.

The Montague Horse, knowing the country so well, were advanced as guides and picket, and hot work we had of it When we got to the Kye, our passage was strongly opposed, even without any opposition. It looked a fearful place. The river flowed rapidly down a deep gully, between two rugged, jagged mountains, a dense bush to the water s edge. One thousand good men could keep twenty thousand from crossing if so disposed; but as nothing ever stopped the progress of British troops, if forward was the word, we forced the passage, after some fighting, and the mounted force, under Tottenham, pushed on to intercept the cattle before they drove them to Zululand, where Pandee was chief. After seven days' hard marching, we reached the Umzuvoola River in front of them, and now, as we had the river behind, and the cattle in front coming up, we expected some severe bush fighting.

This we accomplished, seizing 30,000 head, besides sheep and goats. Many of these cattle had been stolen from our settlers, comprising their entire wealth, and by capturing these we were injuring our enemy as much as in actual war, as the less they had the sooner would they make peace. On returning, they were separated into three droves, with infantry on the flanks, cavalry in rear, Fingoes driving. One drove a day behind the other, one to the left, one to the extreme right on account of the grass, and when halting at night, we lighted fires all around to prevent a stampede, the enemy following us, firing all night, to get a run.

In approaching the River Kye, we had great trouble in keeping them together. They had no water two days, and naturally enough, the brutes were running over each other to get at it. Then the rush down to the water, the confusion caused by the presence of so many, the shouting of all the men in their different dialects, swimming across the river, clambering over rocks on opposite side, the barking of dogs, sheep and goats bleating, hundreds lying down dying, the chasing of others along, trampling on the fallen—such a bedlam and confusion of noises I never before experienced, and heartily wished it all over. After one month's marching, not all so bad, but nearly, as I have just described, we reached headquarters at King William's Town, short 5,000 cattle and sheep, eaten up by the lions, wolves and wild dogs following in our track. As soon as the saved were rested, and it became known to the farmers, all were sold to the farmers at a nominal sum.

Shortly after this affair. Sir Harry Smith was called home. Sir George Cathcart having arrived to take his place. Sandilla, feeling the immense loss of the cattle, came in and surrendered.

The relief which this movement of Sandilla occasioned lasted only a few weeks, news arriving of the uprising of another chief, Moshusha, of the Basautees' country. No news could be more unsatisfactory, as the men hated bush fighting, never having a chance of open, man to man warfare. Pleasant or unpleasant, we marched for his territory. His stronghold we found in a high hill, standing almost alone in a plain, but so covered with prickly pears and cactus as to seem almost impossible to reach. Getting our big guns in position, we played on his fortress with such good effect, it was soon abandoned, and down they came on the plain where the 12th Lancers, after some hard fighting, intercepted their retreat to the Transvaal. Finding it was useless to continue the struggle, their chief capitulated, terms of peace were arranged, and the volunteers returned to Fort William, were disbanded, and returned to their respective homes.

Many had died of dysentery, brought on chiefly through lack of flour for bread. Our living on this route was chiefly on fresh meat and roasted com cobs—no vegetables, and bad water. One instance of the filth and dirty habits of the *kaffirs* I saw on this expedition which I may mention. On the slaughter of a bullock for our use, when the paunch was exposed, filled with green food or fodder, it has invariably been seized and devoured as a luxury, just as it was, hot from the carcase.

This last surrender of the Basantees' chief put an end to the war. All the native and European levies were disbanded, the officers receiving six months' pay for the losses of effects. Each farmer returned to his farm, the merchant to his legitimate business, and the local magistrate, as we had many with us serving in the ranks, to his business. I, with five others, planned an excursion to the Vaal River, intending to trade with the natives for ivory, skins, gum, or anything we could obtain of value, also intending to try our hands at elephant shooting or. hunting. This we found easy to commence, as the merchants of Grahamstown supply all necessary articles for an outfit to the amount of two hundred pounds, should the party pay one-half of the sum, provided on the return you trade the articles you received with them.

We were supplied with a waggon, fourteen oxen loaded with articles to carry on our traffic. Each man mounted a good nag, with a rifle slung across the shoulder, and a Hottentot as a driver of the waggon. We had in it a barrel of flour, a case of brandy, also quinine. Our guns would supply all the animal food required. On approaching a tribe, our policy was to show great respect to the chief, making first for his *kraal*, and as his wives approached, giving them presents of trinkets, such as a string of beads, or a piece of red cloth, this being understood as a friendly offering. We found they are always pleased to meet the trader, and will do all they can to protect him, in hopes of his coming again. Then, again, by acts of kindness such as these, you secure a guide from the chief to conduct you to the next.

After crossing the Vaal, it became necessary to light fires at night, to protect our horses and ourselves from the great number of lions in the country. One always remained on watch, he being relieved once during the night. It is well known lions will not attack an animal tied up for fear of being trapped, nor will they approach a fire, as it dazzles their eyesight. They, however, use an expedient by roaring terrifically, scaring any cattle or horses, expecting a general stampede. This also we had to prepare against, by being always ready to hold the animal in fright.

On reaching the elephant track a bushranger is procured. The best to be got are from the Macatee tribe of *kaffirs*. He starts on a hunt for the spoor or footprint of the beast. We had two of these men, who now took us to the ground most likely to find the herds. On reaching their feeding ground we outspan the oxen; two men stop to guard the waggon, the remaining four start in pursuit of game. As soon as we came on the herd, browsing in a sort of park or plain, the males were on the outside, the females and young in the centre. Our first care was not to be scented; to avoid this we rode to the leeward, and then we drew lots for our separate posts. Number one goes in first; next number plants himself near a tree in sight of number one, and within reach if necessary; the next a certain distance from number two, and so with the last, near number three.

When all are posted, number one moves out stealthily, as near as possible to the greatest male with large tusks—previously I should have said, dismounted—and, without any noise, delivers the shot at the most vulnerable part of his body. As soon as hit, this one blew his trumpet as an alarm and a defiance.

Number one then shows himself more distinctly in front of him, he stamped his feet in wild rage and made a charge. Number one was quickly on horseback, leading on to number two, who delivers his shot, then jumps his horse and leads on to number three. The elephant each time going for the one who last fired, and is on foot, thus follows all in succession, giving the first who fired time to reload. He now, having four different enemies, gets baffled, goes for each separately, till tired, he crushes through the jungle or dense bush on his way, and is easily shot down, falling with an awful thud.

Marking the spot where he lays, the herd is followed, now some miles away, and the same planning is gone through till the hunters have all they require. This is not done without a great deal of danger; coolness is indispensable, also a good horse and guides. When we had thus killed our fourth, we returned to each in succession, cut out the tusks, loaded them on our waggon, and left the carcase for the lions. Our larder, while out, was supplied with plenty of antelope and birds, which swarm in the African jungles. On our return we again visit our tribes, gathering skins, horns, or anything they have for barter, and made tracks for Grahamstown.

The Hottentot holds that the lion never kills a man at once when he has struck him down, unless he is irritated. This would appear to be true, in general, as the following incidents may prove. I may add, there is nothing absolute in history on the subject.

My comrade had one day wounded a lion which had been sneaking after our bullocks, and was in the act of reloading when the lion sprung on him. He stood on ground a little elevated, the animal caught him on the shoulder, and both tumbled to the ground, the lion bellowing heartily close to his head; he then shook him with as much ease as a terrier would a rat. He, remembering after, and as he related it, this shaking produced a sort of stupor, a sort of dreaminess in which he neither felt pain nor terror, though quite conscious of his position and all that was happening. Whatever was the cause of this he could never make out—no sense of horror whatever on seeing the beast, and he in his power.

It led me to think if this unconscious state is produced on all animals who are killed by the *carnivora*, it is a wise provision of Providence for lessening pain. The animal's eye was directed towards me, as I raised my piece to shoot him at a distance of about fifteen yards. My gun missed in both barrels as he sprang on me. Leaving his fallen victim he was despatched by a spear in the hands of a *kaffir*, one of our attendants. A farmer told me that while unyoking his oxen, a lion made a plunge and killed two outright by breaking their spine. Now it seems by this the lion takes quite a different course in despatching the larger animals, and I have thought what can be the reason. Man inspires him with fear, and the lion's natural prudence causes him to suspect some ambuscade, even when man is in his power. Even the Africans allow themselves, the lion's knowledge between the different colour of Europeans and themselves, they are very cautious of the whites.

These excursions often prove fatal to many. Numbers have never been heard of. Whether they fell a prey to the numerous wild animals, whether they were prostrated by fevers so prevalent, or their oxen got the tongue sick from the tsetse flies or other insects so numerous, I could never learn, but many leaving on this sport have never returned.

Travelling in the wilds of Africa during the day the scenery all around is grand in the extreme, and so wild; the different-coloured foliage in the sunbeams, the wild craggy hills covered with thick bush, the roar of the lion occasionally as he scents some antelope or zebra near a river or stream, birds of every colour, monkeys innumerable, while the dense gloom that settles on all at night in the great solitude is indescribable.

On arriving at Grahamstown, our merchant received all our articles, and we retired to Stile's hotel to talk of our adventures and enjoy ourselves as Christians should, making some arrangements as to our future movements. While here we came across many who lived in this way; they are called Winklere; some, by continuing and being lucky, have realised a considerable amount of money, while others, as I have before stated, go, but have never returned.

The *kaffir*s memory is remarkable. He will not forget a bullock he has once seen, and two or three years afterwards he will identify it at once, and without difficulty; they will also remember a white man the same. During the war a man of the Macomos tribe was brought in a prisoner; two years after, when I was through that part of the country and visited Macom, that man recognized me, and spoke of the good treatment he got when a prisoner.

The Dutch Boers of South Africa have become so nomadic in their instincts that even when they are permanently settled in villages they still sleep in their clothes. Moreover, they never dream of indulging in the luxury of candles, but turn in with the setting sun, as they did in their waggons, and they detest the British since the abolition of slavery. They are truly patriarchal, living in large families, and having large flocks of sheep, and herds of cattle. The minister of the Lutheran Church travels from place to place, stopping a month at each, when they have camp-meetings. Then the neighbours assemble from all the surrounding farms, bringing waggons, women and children, also Hottentot servants with them.

When my memory carries me back to the battles in the north-west of India, and I think of the bravery displayed by my comrades in arms, what need to go back to Greek History for heroes. Where is there a nation that has produced greater men than Great Britain, on the field of battle, or in the council. Go back to Poitiers and Agincourt, Blenheim and Malplaquet. Then in the Peninsula, Generals Moore, Nelson, Wellington, Picton, Ponsonby; then again, in India: Lords Clive, Gough, Hardinge, Sir Harry Smith, Havelock, Lawrence, Sir Colin Campbell—a long list of heroes whose names are handed down to future generations. Then go back to the Crimea for a Cathcart, who fell at Inkerman; the gallant charge of the 16th Lancers through three squares of infantry, at Aliwal; and the Sikhs were no mean foe; they acknowledged the prowess of the British; also the death ride of the gallant 600 at Balaclava; the Guards and Light Division, at Inkerman, against fearful odds.

The British soldiers have in most critical times, been surrounded when there seemed no hope of deliverance, yet they have cut their way out, often with heavy loss. Let me remind the reader of the Indian mutiny, of the rebels that had been pampered by the East India Company, how they massacred women and children without mercy, and all hope of saving India seemed gone. Yet that noble man Lawrence went and raised a body of Sikhs and Afghans, our old foes, and with them aided the few Europeans to crush the rebellion, and at the siege of Delhi gained the crowning victory.

Yet there are other heroes as brave. The pioneers in this new country, who have had to face innumerable difficulties, such as the lurking Indian, the wolf, bear and panther in the wild bush, opening up the country and making the wilderness blossom as the rose.

I have often been surprised during my residence in Canada, at the little interest the people here take in our affairs in other parts of the globe. Very few seem to know the extent of the British Empire, or the geographical positions of Bengal, Australia, or the Cape Colony, and seem to forget that the settlers in those other parts of the Empire are brothers of the same flesh and blood, and all from the old sod, English, Scotch and Irish, and that the sun never sets on the British dominions, and the English language is spoken in every land. Where shall we find the land that has sent forth these heroes. Look at the map of the world and you can hardly trace the little spots called the British Isles; yet they are gems in the ocean, and how many good Christian heroes have they sent forth to every clime to battle for the Cross; and the Word of God has been printed in every language.

CHAPTER 12

Back to the Cape

I now left the East, after mature consideration, and went west to Clanwilliam, where I found Mr. Shaw, who has before been introduced in these pages. He had been engaged in the war, having three hundred Hottentots under him. He was a magistrate, lived in a fine brick house, had ten thousand acres of land, was a bachelor, and a jolly good fellow at that. On being asked how he could live alone, his answer immediately was, "Jolly times, jolly times." "I am monarch of all I survey."

Visitors were constant at his place from Cape Town on shooting excursions, game being plentiful and choice on large farms. Besides the raising of cattle, his farm produced fine oranges, wheat, Indian corn, and grapes. Homemade wine and brandy were in abundance. Stopping with him three weeks I started again for the Cape, stopping at night in farm houses, where they gladly receive a visitor. Most of the farms along to the Cape are wine farms, the soil mostly sandy, and the weather being very hot, unfits it for grazing land. I found, on arriving, that I had been reported as killed in the Mackazana bush. Not having any fixed purpose as to my future movements, and meeting here with a comrade officer who, like me, had nothing to do, we, after duly weighing all matters, determined to erect and open an hotel. At this time the Australian gold-fields were drawing largely on the population of Europe, and as the Cape would be the coaling and watering place for vessels; on passage, we christened it "The Australasian."

Soon after opening the *Great Britain* put into port, with seven hundred passengers for Melbourne. Of these we secured one hundred and seventy-six as boarders for the time being. Next along came the *Sarah Sands* from London, with three hundred, after her, the *West Wind* from New York, with six hundred. Of all these we had a good share of boarders, giving them pleasure jaunts to the wine farms of Constancia and the Pearl, and took them around the mountain to see the beautiful scenery in this land of the myrtle and the vine.

There is a weekly market held on Wednesday at the Cape, at which articles brought from Europe are sold. Wines and brandies from Spain and Portugal; perfumes and silks from France; linens, calicoes, and broadcloths, also, ready-made clothing from England. This market commences at six in the morning. Farmers' waggons arrive during the night before. Everything is sold after the Dutch fashion. Waggons are arranged in line according to the article for sale. Grain, first line of waggons; vegetables, second; and fruit of all kinds in the third line. The Hottentot boys are the drivers of the yoke, having for an ornament in their caps splendid ostrich feathers. Ostrich eggs or feathers can be had from these boys for sixpence each; they picking them up on the sand can afford to sell cheap. Fish at the Cape is very plentiful and good, and easily caught by line. Lobsters, by dozens, can be brought up by putting a piece of liver in a basket weighted with stones, attached to a rope—lower, in five minutes pull up. I have done this myself.

Off Port Elizabeth a large business is done in whale oil. Taking a trip in a boat belonging to a firm engaged in this business, named Seawright, I saw the whole process of catching and extracting the oil. The Bird Islands are in the Mosambique Channel, and here the sea elephant, as it is called, is plentiful; the animal is amphibious. The men go out at night when it is time for these animals to quit the sea for the shore; when well up on the sand, they noiselessly creep between them and the water, then they are attacked with clubs and beaten to death; if he escapes to water again he carries with him anything in his way, but only to secure a good ducking. Thirty or forty will thus be killed in one night by eight or nine men; the blubber is boiled down into oil, and sent to the Cape. These animals are the size of a good land pig, with tusks like elephants—a species of whale, though commonly called sea elephants.

The Island abounds with rabbits and goats, and a curious bird may be found here called the "Penguin." They never use their wings, but march upright in flocks like a company of soldiers. Seeing them at a distance, as they are large, and having a red spot on the breast, they might be taken for a company of soldiers. If, in walking, you meet with a thousand they never get out of the way, you may do as you please, but they only peck at you. I stayed at the islands three days while the ship was being freighted with oil, and on returning to the Cape I mightily enjoyed the sail on the beautiful calm sea in this southern hemisphere—the whale spouting, and the golden dolphin swimming around the boat.

As we neared the Cape, better known to me now, and as it was after four in the afternoon, no one could be seen on the streets, but many under the stoops of their houses, in the cool, sleeping. All outdoor work is over at ten in the morning; after five in the evening all is bustle and life again—ladies promenading the Kesingraf, or ladies' walk. The road from the town leading to Newlands through Rondebosch, is very pleasant—trees on both sides for eight or nine miles. The clergyman of the English church at Newlands showed me a collection of animals he had for the then Lord Derby, some fine specimens of eland, giraffe, and gazelle, the smallest of the deer species; he had also a lion and a panther. The heavy rolls from the Atlantic set in early in winter, and during the season no vessels venture into the bay; if they got safely in there they should remain until spring.

The weather on land is very pleasant during this time—much like an English autumn. In November, a bark from Baltimore, in the States, bound to Bombay, came ashore on Robbin Island a wreck; a number went off to assist the crew; on reaching the rocks the captain and a number of sailors had got ashore—his wife, two children, and the mate were missing. The captain was nearly out of his mind through the loss, they were found the next day—two beautiful girls—and I can never forget the man's looks as he saw them laid out for burial. The wife was found under the keel of the vessel, and the mate jammed between the casks of porter in the hold. It was a melancholy funeral.

I will now revert to my travels in Kaffraria, to mention some things interesting which I omitted then. In commencing, I may say that the meaning of *kaffir* is thief, by calling men of some tribes who know this, they are very indignant. They generally have from three to six wives, who do all the laborious work, even to building the hut for herself, my lord going into which he pleases. They do all the gardening, sow corn, plant pumpkins and other vegetables, milk cows and cook, the boys helping, and are never allowed to eat with the men; these latter attend to the cattle until eighteen, when they are circumcised and allowed to sit with the warriors and hunt with them.

When he has arrived at the period of manhood to marry, he selects a wife, the chief and councillors set a price on her according to her charms, say, two cows or three heifers, and if he does not possess so much he will steal from the nearest settler or from another tribe; this occurring often is the cause of much war between the several tribes. One day a fine young fellow named Magesa, a chief's son of the Patos tribe, came to me, pulling a long face. He said he wanted a girl of another tribe, but he had not her value, nor would his father give him the cow and two heifers he required, as he wanted to buy another wife for himself. This boy previously had done me a good turn, and feeling for him, as well as to prevent him from stealing, I got the required cattle which he accepted.

He brought his bride afterwards to thank me. I was surprised, however, when he made a request for a row of beads to decorate her neck, and also for a plug of tobacco with which to console himself. These I gave him, and in return the high favour of kissing the newly married lady was imposed upon me. Their clothing being very scant, and all procured by hunting the deer, don't cost much, but their begging propensities are very great, for a chief with four wives and five hundred head of cattle would beg as this lad had done.

There is very little emigration to the Cape, the reason is,

capital is required. Labour is so cheap, no white man will engage in it for a living. Land can be purchased, worked to advantage, either in grain, or stock-farming, and this requires means. The principal export is merino wool. The native sheep are like goats, with hair. They have extraordinary large tails, all fat. I have seen a tail as large as the carcase.

In consequence of the loss of my wife and child by smallpox, brought to the Cape in a slaver captured on the west coast, and the defalcations of my partner in the hotel business, through which he absconded to Australia with one thousand pounds of our money, I was compelled to resign my business and return to England. A vessel on her way from Calcutta, putting in for water, I took passage, and bid goodbye to the Cape. The voyage was a rough one, we encountered many storms, arriving safe at the East India Docks on 24th March, 1855, after a voyage of ten weeks.

I immediately left for Buckinghamshire, where my family had removed during my absence, and found, to my great sorrow, my poor mother had been dead just two months, her last words were: "Oh, that I could but see my dear son before I am called away." My father, feeling this affliction deeply, having lived together some forty-six years, soon followed her, and I had had that consolation of being present when he died, and laid him beside my dear angel mother. After arranging some family matters at our old home, I left for London, expecting to get a commission in the Turkish contingent, from Lord Panmure. While waiting for this, peace was proclaimed, and the troops ordered home from the Crimea.

Notwithstanding all the excitement caused by that war, my services were not forgotten, though, perhaps, in the eyes of some, the famous charge of the Six Hundred, had eclipsed Aliwal and Sobraon, still I had a good friend in the Marquis of Chandos, who gave me the appointment of station-master on the London and North-Western Railway below Rugby, where I remained till 1859. In the month of November, 1859, a serious accident occurred on my section of this road, which might have been more serious for me, as I was only recently appointed, had I not used the caution on the moment I did, showing my training as a soldier was useful even on a railroad.

About three in the afternoon, the Midland Express, twenty minutes overdue, a mineral train came along. I cautioned the driver to get clear as quickly as possible, which he did, till about three hundred yards from the station he broke down. I immediately telegraphed "line blocked." Soon the Express, late, came in sight, thundering along under two engines—twelve carriages and two guard vans. Trying all means, I could not stop it, danger signal was up, waved red flag, still on she came at a rate of seventy miles an hour. As they passed me, still waving and shouting, they screwed down to twenty miles; but on she went into the mineral train, smashing the engine and telescoping the carriages. Fortunately a down train for Aylesbury had just passed the freight train, or it would have been much worse. As it was, I felt much worse than ever I did when charging up to the mouth of a big gun at Magarajpoor, or charging square of Sikhs, at Aliwal. There were many of the passengers wounded, one, a lady's maid, was killed. The wounded were removed to a gentleman's residence nearby. Lord and Lady Byron were slightly injured.

The Board of Directors of course had an investigation to which I was summoned, but completely exonerated from all blame, as it was proved the station-master below me had neglected his duty, in not seeing my telegraph "line blocked." I received great praise from the London papers, and was promoted by the Board to a more responsible and lucrative post. Still I never could feel happy on my post. My wife—having married again—constantly fretted for fear of a repetition, and as it was a worry to my mind, I resigned as I have before stated, in 1859.

I then went to Liverpool to fill an appointment as Drill Instructor to the Exchange corps of Volunteers, under Captain Bright, and in that city I remained, until the opening of the Great Exhibition, in 1862, when I got an appointment in the first great world's show. When it closed I went to Hampstead, where I was college drill-master until 1869, when I left for Brighton, my birthplace, as superintendent of the Grand Hotel. So many early associations connected with this place, and as I had lost all my relatives nearly, I made up my mind to remove to America along with an old friend of mine, who determined, like me, to anchor at last in the New World.

Having now reached the point of the story of my life when I must bid farewell to my reader, I feel refreshed—life renewed almost in having gone over the history of my early connection with the army, and the subsequent perils, combats, and adventures in which I was engaged. I can scarcely credit, on looking back, that all such has occurred, and that I am the same who, so many years ago, toiled under great disadvantages through the hot sands of India, parched with thirst, and ill-provided with food fit for such a climate. I sometimes think if it is possible, or is a long-past dream—the charges on Sikh squares at Aliwal and Sobraon, the storming of huge works, the capture of citadels, the marching in triumph through many a proud eastern city, after teaching their arrogant rulers that treachery or treason could not be tolerated by the British. Did I once stand on the steps of the throne of the once powerful Moguls of Delhi, and assist at the capture, and escort, after toilsome marches, some of the turbulent princes of India; and in all these had the honour of serving under such soldiers as Hardinge, Gough, Pollock, Nott, Smith, Havelock, and a Cathcart. Apart from this, in another continent, hunting the huge elephant in the jungles, the slow, stealthy creep to the leeward of the beast—the shot—the roar—the crash into the thicket—the double shot—and eventually the heavy thud with which he falls to the earth almost lifeless.

It has often been said, "*Once a soldier, always a soldier,*" and another common saying equally as true, "*It runs in the blood.*" These assertions are true as far as my experience has led me to judge. I am but a poor example of the truth. One has only to read over the names of our country's heroes, and, tracing them for generations back, their ancestors have mostly belonged to either branch of Her Majesty's service. I am now in the sere and yellow leaf, but would tomorrow, if not so incapacitated heartily join my old comrades—"*The Pride of England—the Terror of India,*" ready to go over the same ground again. This cannot be, however. We all have our day; young men are coming to the front every day, animated with the same spirit, but, it seems to me, possessed with more caution. They, no doubt, when called, will emulate the example of their predecessors in deeds of bravery.

The Peninsular War, ending at Waterloo, produced brave and heroic men, who have left their names on the scroll of fame. The Sikh war added another long list, in which Aliwal and Sobraon heroes figure conspicuously, as did also the Maharratta War. Again, the Crimea, with its terrible charge of the Six Hundred, and the dreadful sufferings through the severe winter of 1854 and 1855, will never be forgotten. Then the Indian Mutiny, where our countrymen's names come in with those of Sir Colin and Havelock, for a high meed of praise—all showing that in the breasts of the sons of the "Three Kingdoms" there is born a living fire, which, when kindled on the cry of the oppressed or downtrodden of earth will burn till liberty and freedom is enthroned.

God Save the Queen.

LEONAUR

ALSO FROM LEONAUR

AVAILABLE IN SOFTCOVER OR HARDCOVER WITH DUST JACKET

AT THEM WITH THE BAYONET *by Donald F. Featherstone*—The first Anglo-Sikh War 1845-1846.

STEPHEN CRANE'S BATTLES *by Stephen Crane*—Nine Decisive Battles Recounted by the Author of 'The Red Badge of Courage'.

THE GURKHA WAR *by H. T. Prinsep*—The Anglo-Nepalese Conflict in North East India 1814-1816.

FIRE & BLOOD *by G. R. Gleig*—The burning of Washington & the battle of New Orleans, 1814, through the eyes of a young British soldier.

SOUND ADVANCE! *by Joseph Anderson*—Experiences of an officer of HM 50th regiment in Australia, Burma & the Gwalior war.

THE CAMPAIGN OF THE INDUS *by Thomas Holdsworth*—Experiences of a British Officer of the 2nd (Queen's Royal) Regiment in the Campaign to Place Shah Shuja on the Throne of Afghanistan 1838 - 1840.

WITH THE MADRAS EUROPEAN REGIMENT IN BURMA *by John Butler*—The Experiences of an Officer of the Honourable East India Company's Army During the First Anglo-Burmese War 1824 - 1826.

IN ZULULAND WITH THE BRITISH ARMY *by Charles L. Norris-Newman*—The Anglo-Zulu war of 1879 through the first-hand experiences of a special correspondent.

BESIEGED IN LUCKNOW *by Martin Richard Gubbins*—The first Anglo-Sikh War 1845-1846.

A TIGER ON HORSEBACK *by L. March Phillips*—The Experiences of a Trooper & Officer of Rimington's Guides - The Tigers - during the Anglo-Boer war 1899 - 1902.

SEPOYS, SIEGE & STORM *by Charles John Griffiths*—The Experiences of a young officer of H.M.'s 61st Regiment at Ferozepore, Delhi ridge and at the fall of Delhi during the Indian mutiny 1857.

CAMPAIGNING IN ZULULAND *by W. E. Montague*—Experiences on campaign during the Zulu war of 1879 with the 94th Regiment.

THE STORY OF THE GUIDES *by G.J. Younghusband*—The Exploits of the Soldiers of the famous Indian Army Regiment from the northwest frontier 1847 - 1900.

LEONAUR

ALSO FROM LEONAUR
AVAILABLE IN SOFTCOVER OR HARDCOVER WITH DUST JACKET

OFFICERS & GENTLEMEN *by Peter Hawker & William Graham*—Two Accounts of British Officers During the Peninsula War: Officer of Light Dragoons by Peter Hawker & Campaign in Portugal and Spain by William Graham .

THE WALCHEREN EXPEDITION *by Anonymous*—The Experiences of a British Officer of the 81st Regt. During the Campaign in the Low Countries of 1809.

LADIES OF WATERLOO *by Charlotte A. Eaton, Magdalene de Lancey & Juana Smith*—The Experiences of Three Women During the Campaign of 1815: Waterloo Days by Charlotte A. Eaton, A Week at Waterloo by Magdalene de Lancey & Juana's Story by Juana Smith.

JOURNAL OF AN OFFICER IN THE KING'S GERMAN LEGION *by John Frederick Hering*—Recollections of Campaigning During the Napoleonic Wars.

JOURNAL OF AN ARMY SURGEON IN THE PENINSULAR WAR *by Charles Boutflower*—The Recollections of a British Army Medical Man on Campaign During the Napoleonic Wars.

ON CAMPAIGN WITH MOORE AND WELLINGTON *by Anthony Hamilton*—The Experiences of a Soldier of the 43rd Regiment During the Peninsular War.

THE ROAD TO AUSTERLITZ *by R. G. Burton*—Napoleon's Campaign of 1805.

SOLDIERS OF NAPOLEON *by A. J. Doisy De Villargennes & Arthur Chuquet*—The Experiences of the Men of the French First Empire: Under the Eagles by A. J. Doisy De Villargennes & Voices of 1812 by Arthur Chuquet .

INVASION OF FRANCE, 1814 *by F. W. O. Maycock*—The Final Battles of the Napoleonic First Empire.

LEIPZIG—A CONFLICT OF TITANS *by Frederic Shoberl*—A Personal Experience of the 'Battle of the Nations' During the Napoleonic Wars, October 14th-19th, 1813.

SLASHERS *by Charles Cadell*—The Campaigns of the 28th Regiment of Foot During the Napoleonic Wars by a Serving Officer.

BATTLE IMPERIAL *by Charles William Vane*—The Campaigns in Germany & France for the Defeat of Napoleon 1813-1814.

SWIFT & BOLD *by Gibbes Rigaud*—The 60th Rifles During the Peninsula War.

LEONAUR

ALSO FROM LEONAUR
AVAILABLE IN SOFTCOVER OR HARDCOVER WITH DUST JACKET

ADVENTURES OF A YOUNG RIFLEMAN *by Johann Christian Maempel*—The Experiences of a Saxon in the French & British Armies During the Napoleonic Wars.

THE HUSSAR *by Norbert Landsheit & G. R. Gleig*—A German Cavalryman in British Service Throughout the Napoleonic Wars.

RECOLLECTIONS OF THE PENINSULA *by Moyle Sherer*—An Officer of the 34th Regiment of Foot—'The Cumberland Gentlemen'—on Campaign Against Napoleon's French Army in Spain.

MARINE OF REVOLUTION & CONSULATE *by Moreau de Jonnès*—The Recollections of a French Soldier of the Revolutionary Wars 1791-1804.

GENTLEMEN IN RED *by John Dobbs & Robert Knowles*—Two Accounts of British Infantry Officers During the Peninsular War Recollections of an Old 52nd Man by John Dobbs An Officer of Fusiliers by Robert Knowles.

CORPORAL BROWN'S CAMPAIGNS IN THE LOW COUNTRIES *by Robert Brown*—Recollections of a Coldstream Guard in the Early Campaigns Against Revolutionary France 1793-1795.

THE 7TH (QUEENS OWN) HUSSARS: Volume 2—1793-1815 *by C. R. B. Barrett*—During the Campaigns in the Low Countries & the Peninsula and Waterloo Campaigns of the Napoleonic Wars. Volume 2: 1793-1815.

THE MARENGO CAMPAIGN 1800 *by Herbert H. Sargent*—The Victory that Completed the Austrian Defeat in Italy.

DONALDSON OF THE 94TH—SCOTS BRIGADE *by Joseph Donaldson*—The Recollections of a Soldier During the Peninsula & South of France Campaigns of the Napoleonic Wars.

A CONSCRIPT FOR EMPIRE *by Philippe as told to Johann Christian Maempel*—The Experiences of a Young German Conscript During the Napoleonic Wars.

JOURNAL OF THE CAMPAIGN OF 1815 *by Alexander Cavalié Mercer*—The Experiences of an Officer of the Royal Horse Artillery During the Waterloo Campaign.

NAPOLEON'S CAMPAIGNS IN POLAND 1806-7 *by Robert Wilson*—The campaign in Poland from the Russian side of the conflict.

LEONAUR

ALSO FROM LEONAUR
AVAILABLE IN SOFTCOVER OR HARDCOVER WITH DUST JACKET

THE LIFE OF THE REAL BRIGADIER GERARD VOLUME 1—THE YOUNG HUSSAR 1782-1807 *by Jean-Baptiste De Marbot*—A French Cavalryman Of the Napoleonic Wars at Marengo, Austerlitz, Jena, Eylau & Friedland.

THE LIFE OF THE REAL BRIGADIER GERARD VOLUME 2—IMPERIAL AIDE-DE-CAMP 1807-1811 *by Jean-Baptiste De Marbot*—A French Cavalryman of the Napoleonic Wars at Saragossa, Landshut, Eckmuhl, Ratisbon, Aspern-Essling, Wagram, Busaco & Torres Vedras.

THE LIFE OF THE REAL BRIGADIER GERARD VOLUME 3—COLONEL OF CHASSEURS 1811-1815 *by Jean-Baptiste De Marbot*—A French Cavalryman in the retreat from Moscow, Lutzen, Bautzen, Katzbach, Leipzig, Hanau & Waterloo.

THE INDIAN WAR OF 1864 *by Eugene Ware*—The Experiences of a Young Officer of the 7th Iowa Cavalry on the Western Frontier During the Civil War.

THE MARCH OF DESTINY *by Charles E. Young & V. Devinny*—Dangers of the Trail in 1865 by Charles E. Young & The Story of a Pioneer by V. Devinny, two Accounts of Early Emigrants to Colorado.

CROSSING THE PLAINS *by William Audley Maxwell*—A First Hand Narrative of the Early Pioneer Trail to California in 1857.

CHIEF OF SCOUTS *by William F. Drannan*—A Pilot to Emigrant and Government Trains, Across the Plains of the Western Frontier.

THIRTY-ONE YEARS ON THE PLAINS AND IN THE MOUNTAINS *by William F. Drannan*—William Drannan was born to be a pioneer, hunter, trapper and wagon train guide during the momentous days of the Great American West.

THE INDIAN WARS VOLUNTEER *by William Thompson*—Recollections of the Conflict Against the Snakes, Shoshone, Bannocks, Modocs and Other Native Tribes of the American North West.

THE 4TH TENNESSEE CAVALRY *by George B. Guild*—The Services of Smith's Regiment of Confederate Cavalry by One of its Officers.

COLONEL WORTHINGTON'S SHILOH *by T. Worthington*—The Tennessee Campaign, 1862, by an Officer of the Ohio Volunteers.

FOUR YEARS IN THE SADDLE *by W. L. Curry*—The History of the First Regiment Ohio Volunteer Cavalry in the American Civil War.

LEONAUR

ALSO FROM LEONAUR
AVAILABLE IN SOFTCOVER OR HARDCOVER WITH DUST JACKET

THE 9TH—THE KING'S (LIVERPOOL REGIMENT) IN THE GREAT WAR 1914 - 1918 *by Enos H. G. Roberts*—Mersey to mud—war and Liverpool men.

THE GAMBARDIER *by Mark Severn*—The experiences of a battery of Heavy artillery on the Western Front during the First World War.

FROM MESSINES TO THIRD YPRES *by Thomas Floyd*—A personal account of the First World War on the Western front by a 2/5th Lancashire Fusilier.

THE IRISH GUARDS IN THE GREAT WAR - VOLUME 1 *by Rudyard Kipling*—Edited and Compiled from Their Diaries and Papers—The First Battalion.

THE IRISH GUARDS IN THE GREAT WAR - VOLUME 1 *by Rudyard Kipling*—Edited and Compiled from Their Diaries and Papers—The Second Battalion.

ARMOURED CARS IN EDEN *by K. Roosevelt*—An American President's son serving in Rolls Royce armoured cars with the British in Mesopatamia & with the American Artillery in France during the First World War.

CHASSEUR OF 1914 *by Marcel Dupont*—Experiences of the twilight of the French Light Cavalry by a young officer during the early battles of the great war in Europe.

TROOP HORSE & TRENCH *by R.A. Lloyd*—The experiences of a British Lifeguardsman of the household cavalry fighting on the western front during the First World War 1914-18.

THE EAST AFRICAN MOUNTED RIFLES *by C.J. Wilson*—Experiences of the campaign in the East African bush during the First World War.

THE LONG PATROL *by George Berrie*—A Novel of Light Horsemen from Gallipoli to the Palestine campaign of the First World War.

THE FIGHTING CAMELIERS *by Frank Reid*—The exploits of the Imperial Camel Corps in the desert and Palestine campaigns of the First World War.

STEEL CHARIOTS IN THE DESERT *by S. C. Rolls*—The first world war experiences of a Rolls Royce armoured car driver with the Duke of Westminster in Libya and in Arabia with T.E. Lawrence.

WITH THE IMPERIAL CAMEL CORPS IN THE GREAT WAR *by Geoffrey Inchbald*—The story of a serving officer with the British 2nd battalion against the Senussi and during the Palestine campaign.

www.ingramcontent.com/pod-product-compliance
Lightning Source LLC
Chambersburg PA
CBHW031900090426
42741CB00005B/581